# The Evolutionary Leap
## toward Flourishing Organizations

Center for Evolutionary Learning (CEL)
 Frank Bruck
 Michela Cavalletti
 Calin Costian
 Wolfgang Hackl
 Gregoire de Kalbermatten

*Scientific advisor*
 Maurizio Zollo

*Editorial team*
 Calin Costian
 Gregoire de Kalbermatten
 Maurizio Zollo

# THE EVOLUTIONARY LEAP

## TO FLOURISHING INDIVIDUALS AND ORGANIZATIONS

LONDON AND NEW YORK

First published 2017
by Routledge
2 Park Square, Milton Park, Abingdon, Oxon OX14 4RN

and by Routledge
711 Third Avenue, New York, NY 10017

Routledge is an imprint of the Taylor & Francis Group, an informa business

© 2017 Routledge

The rights of the Authors of this work to be identified as such has been asserted by them in accordance with sections 77 and 78 of the Copyright, Designs and Patents Act 1988.

All rights reserved. No part of this book may be reprinted or reproduced or utilised in any form or by any electronic, mechanical, or other means, now known or hereafter invented, including photocopying and recording, or in any information storage or retrieval system, without permission in writing from the publishers.

Trademark notice: Product or corporate names may be trademarks or registered trademarks, and are used only for identification and explanation without intent to infringe.

*British Library Cataloguing-in-Publication Data*
A catalogue record for this book is available from the British Library.

*Library of Congress Cataloging-in-Publication Data*
A catalog record for this book has been requested.

ISBN: 978-1-78353-781-5 (hbk)
ISBN: 978-1-78353-799-0 (pbk)
ISBN: 978-1-78353-783-9 (ebk)

Cover design: Soham Dhingra

# Contents

About the authors ... vii
Acknowledgments ... x
Introduction ... 1

**Part I: The Premise** ... 7
   1: The challenge ... 9
   2: The leap in the field ... 21

**Part II: Individual Flourishing** ... 55
   3: The neuroscientific evidence ... 57
   4: The inner transformation engine ... 75
   5: The field of collective consciousness ... 113

**Part III: Toward the Flourishing Organization** ... 129
   6: The transition models of organizations ... 131
   7: Practical steps for the transition ... 149

Conclusions ... 171
Glossary ... 179
Bibliography ... 181
Endnotes ... 185

# About the authors

This book is the result of a collective effort by many of the founding partners of the Center for Evolutionary Learning (CEL), a global network of business professionals representing over 40 countries. Since 2005, CEL has helped organizations evolve towards higher models of performance, sustainability and social responsibility. Its client list includes HP, IBM, Microsoft, Shell, the United Nations and many other corporations, and governmental and inter-governmental institutions.

**Frank Bruck** is an academic researcher and educator, holds a doctoral degree in social and economic sciences from Vienna University of Economics and Business (WU Vienna), and is currently the managing director of the global sustainability research network (GOLDEN) and a senior researcher at Bocconi University in Italy. For over 25 years he has been working as a trainer, consultant, and coach for European companies, notably in the areas of intercultural competence, management, and corporate social responsibility. As the head of the International Studies Center at WU Vienna, he acquired negotiation experience in more than 40 countries. Frank currently lives in Cape Town, South Africa, where he is director of Be The Change Consulting and visiting professor at the Graduate School of Business, University of Cape Town. He is a founding member and director on the board of CEL International and an author of numerous academic publications. Frank is married and has four children.

**Michela Cavalletti** has a Master's degree in political science from the University of Perugia in Italy and a postgraduate degree as Manager for Development Projects. She has (i) worked in a managerial capacity with NGOs (on development projects and international partnerships), (ii) completed several assignments for governmental and nongovernmental (NGO) agencies in Africa and Eastern Europe, and (iii) monitored and evaluated projects funded by the European Union. Her main interests include emerging economies, corporate governance, human resources, and evolutionary training (e.g., gender issues). She is a director on the board of CEL International, is married with three children, and lives in Perugia, Italy.

**Calin Costian** is a telecom and IT executive with over 20 years of experience in strategic pricing, presales enablement, commercial marketing, engineering, and operations. His primary field of focus is sales cycle acceleration and revenue and profit optimization for global enterprises. A native of Romania, he holds advanced degrees in Mathematics (University of Bucharest) and Computer Sciences (Purdue University) where he was a Purdue Research Foundation Fellow funded by the National Science Foundation. He has authored numerous articles across a broad spectrum of topics from business to mathematics and computer sciences, has served on the boards of American and global non-profit organizations, and is currently Chairman and President of CEL International. He lives in Dallas, Texas with his wife and two children.

**Wolfgang Hackl** is a trainer, speaker, consultant, and coach. For more than 20 years he has inspired and aided corporations and institutions primarily in Europe, and in the US and South America as well. He has established his own business training and coaching company, "Impact," in 2003. Besides his MA in psychology, education, and philosophy, and PhD in the science of sports, Wolfgang Hackl has a number of colorful items on his CV. He has been a singer in musicals and opera, an international model, ski instructor, organizer of scuba diving expeditions in the Maldives, and participant in European windsurfing championships. He is a founding member and director on the board of CEL International and lives in Vienna, Austria with his wife and three children.

**Gregoire de Kalbermatten** completed his law degree (Geneva) with postgraduate degrees in international relations (SAIS Bologna) and political science at Johns Hopkins University in Baltimore (where he was a fellow of the university president). A diplomat of his country (Switzerland), Gregoire has served at a senior level in the United Nations—in the fields of capital investment, economic development, and environment protection. He has directed, co-authored, and published a number of related books, reports and studies; led over 300 missions on the five continents; prepared numerous intergovernmental events (e.g., ministerial conferences and scientific symposiums); and maintains a keen interest in the philosophy of history, world cultures and global affairs. Gregoire is a founding member and director on the board of CEL International. He and his wife live near Geneva and have three children and four grandchildren.

**Maurizio Zollo** has a PhD in management from the Wharton School, University of Pennsylvania. He served for 10 years on the faculty of INSEAD's strategy department and is presently the Dean's Chaired Professor in Strategy and Sustainability at the Management and Technology department of Bocconi University, Milan. Former President of the European Academy of Management, he is a visiting professor in the Management Science Group of the Sloan School of Management at MIT, Boston. The author of more than 50 academic publications and three books which have received several awards and over 11,000 citations, he is also the chief editor of *Organization and Environment*, a leading academic journal specialized in corporate sustainability, and the Scientific Director of the Global Organizational Learning and Development Network for Sustainability (GOLDEN—www.goldenforsustainability.com). He is married and lives with his wife and daughter in Milan, Italy.

# Acknowledgments

The innovative ideas in this book have matured over decades of scientific research (in management, medical, and neurosciences) and training, coaching, and consulting undertaken by many of the contributors and authors of this work. Nonetheless, the ideas are still considered experimental hypotheses and statements and thus must be validated by the direct experience of business managers and their respective organizations. In actuality, this book is a *call to experimentation*. We emphasize the fact that such organizational innovations are based on unique combinations of mindsets, value systems and cognitive/emotional schemas. Those who have chosen earlier (and will choose in the future) to experiment with the advocated approaches are, in a true sense, co-developers of this evolving praxis.

The specific purpose and logic of this book emerged from a brainstorming session with directors and instructors of the Center for Evolutionary Learning (CEL) in Italy and was subsequently developed through the authoring and editing work of a number of CEL board members and scientific advisors. The contributions of the authors are based on their specific domains of expertise; however, the blending of knowledge across all chapters has resulted in the present book being a truly collective work as opposed to a sequential compilation of individual contributions.

We recognize the authoring contributions of Frank Bruck, Michela Cavalletti, Calin Costian, Wolfgang Hackl, Gregoire de Kalbermatten and the scientific guidance of Maurizio Zollo. We also thank Dr.

Ivano Ferri, Valeria Berchicci, Kris Vander Velpen, and all those who provided inputs and guidance. Likewise, we appreciate the advice and comments of Chris Laszlo and Sandra Waddock, as well as Benoit de Bellefroid, Stefano Sedola, and Rahul Rai. We acknowledge the cutting-edge research of Dr. Katya Rubia from King's College in London, which was foundational in laying the neuroscientific basis of some of the insights in this book. We are grateful to Jill Westfall for copyediting assistance, to Soham Dhingra for the cover design, and to Herbert Reininger for the overall graphic design help. Our special words of thanks go to Greenleaf Publishing for bringing this project to light.

This book is dedicated to the fond memory of a globally recognized speaker and spiritual guide, Shri Mataji Nirmala Devi. She revealed the inner workings of a mechanism enabling the individual and collective evolution that promotes an elevated state of consciousness, perception, and ability to perfect oneself, which is at the heart of the evolutionary leap to individual and organizational flourishing.

# Introduction

"If everyone is thinking alike, then no one is thinking."

**Benjamin Franklin**

The last thing the world needs is yet another book delineating corporation-induced dangers and damages such as environmental disequilibria, social inequalities, and unethical conduct. Over the past few decades, such issues have been powerfully described through rigorous scientific work. Therefore, the addition of new arguments is likely to be at best only marginally useful, and at worst downright futile. Still, these problems persist and are increasingly deep, complex, and urgent according to most expert observers. In fact, there are currently widespread questions about the fundamentals of business activity and how organizations should be established and managed.

We see the debate among managers, academics, policymakers and private citizens shifting from *problem definitions* to *solution identifications*—and, most importantly, execution. Fortunately, there is no shortage of ideas on what the endgame might look like in terms of the sustainability requirements of business activities. In fact, there are (i) plenty of models that characterize the enterprise as an entity that integrates the interests of a plurality of internal and external stakeholders (into its core values, culture, governance, strategies, and processes); (ii) technologies to monitor and reduce the environmental impact of business operations (both within and across value chains);

and (iii) shared value logics, circular logistics, and shared economy models—to name a few of the best-known concepts in private and public discourse. Many companies are fully committed to figuring out what such ideas might mean for their organizations, and even trying out some of the tools to enhance the quality of their social and environmental impacts while strengthening their innovative processes and revenue base.

Still, the problem is not going away. The way we run (and conceive of) businesses today has generally not changed materially, with rare exceptions in environmental practices, human resource management, and supply chain engagement. Thus, there is little mitigation in environmental damage and social injustices across industries and value chains. For these reasons, there are hindrances associated with organizational and systemic evolutions—changes that are generally acknowledged as necessary for managing, regulating, funding, and observing business activities.

In the present book we offer a number of suggestions on how to move forward and address these issues. To begin with, we need to rethink the concept of sustainability, which we hold should not be limited to the reduction of environmental or social damage as it is implicitly or explicitly conceived of today. Rather, it should be about (i) making a *net positive impact* on society and the natural environment[1] and (ii) nurturing the full realization of human potential—in harmony with other species on the planet. John Ehrenfeld[2] (one of the pioneers of the notion of sustainability decades ago) has explored the concept of "sustainability-as-flourishing," which he defines as *"the possibility that humans and other life will flourish on the Earth forever."* The achievement of sustainability-as-flourishing requires nothing less than nurturing and realizing the fullest potential of individuals and organizations.

How do we understand—and enact—this transformation? Even the correct framing of sustainability-associated challenges does not imply that we know how to enact a deep transformation within the mindsets of business managers, as well as the purpose, governance, and operating processes of their organizations.

We wrote this book precisely to offer an answer to this question. We would like to submit our proposed answer to the scientific debate on corporate and global sustainability, regard it as a testable hypothesis and submit that it should also be tested in the context of ongoing business practices—by managers, entrepreneurs, and leaders of for-profit and non-profit organizations. If validated, it is our hope that it will be considered worthy of support by policymakers, political party officers, civil society frontrunners, and by all concerned, discriminating individuals who are interested in the future development of economic and social welfare.

The answer lies in the notion of "evolutionary leaps" in human consciousness. Such rapid and at the same time profound changes can yield integrative awareness, experiences, decision-making and actions in all spheres of life, including business, that are spontaneously directed towards promoting the common good. They also lead to an expansion of the notion of identity to a collective level through the experience and development of this new dimension of awareness. This state of consciousness has been identified and characterized by increasingly precise neural correlates, which have been recently shown in scientific experiments to have a strong correlation with sustainable decision-making (i.e., based on longer time horizons and a willingness to forego immediate individual rewards for larger collective ones).

How is this evolutionary leap to a flourishing state to be achieved? Also, how would consciousness development—at the level of the individual—influence organizational evolution and generate a collective flourishing state? This book is centered on the presentation of answers and explanations associated with these fundamental and yet novel questions.

The first section of the book is dedicated to framing its premise. In the first chapter, we elaborate on the challenges before us and provide a roadmap for (i) tackling these challenges and (ii) generating testable propositions (regarding the role of meditative practices that enable individuals and organizations to develop sustainability-as-flourishing behaviors). Chapter 2 introduces a set of case studies with results that support the effectiveness of the methods we propose.

The second section of the book focuses on arguments that support the proposed role of meditative practices in the achievement of individual flourishing. Two very different—albeit highly complementary—approaches are provided to explain the basis of our arguments. The first one leverages the growing volume of neuroscience research with evidence on the effectiveness of meditation in activating critical areas of the brain that influence sustainable decisions and actions. Recent evidence also shows that deep meditative practices have strong neuroplasticity effects and significantly promote the development of gray matter (i.e., density of neural connectivity) present in the aforementioned brain regions.

The second approach relies on a combined and integrated approach drawing from several wisdom traditions that represent both Eastern and Western civilizations. They are centered on the development of different types of meditative practices and have helped individuals attain higher levels of consciousness that can spontaneously generate virtuous thoughts and behaviors. Chapters 4 and 5 are dedicated to the explanation of the "inner engine" that powers the development of our consciousness.

In the third section of the book, we tackle the second question which is related to the diffusion of individual flourishing states as a means of achieving of organizational flourishing. The use of meditative practices as a personal development tool (as opposed to merely for stress management or wellbeing) is already a significant challenge in most companies; however, even a complete diffusion process is not sufficient for attaining a state of organizational flourishing. To that end, meditative practices must be embedded and leveraged in (i) day-to-day work, (ii) decision-making routines, and (iii) project management processes.

Chapter 6 develops a conceptual framework for envisioning how a flourishing organization might work and thrive. Chapter 7 shares actionable steps that can be undertaken by managers who are willing to engage in transformation and learning processes that enable the emergence of flourishing individuals and organizations. Our "compass" will provide general directions and key milestones for enabling evolutionary leaps in individuals and organizations via integrated change processes. The proposed framework and narrative are complemented by concrete examples and case studies.

The brief concluding chapter summarizes the core thesis of the book and calls for collective action which involves testing the propositions offered in Chapter 1 and sharing the processes necessary for attaining the next logical step in this evolutionary journey: the realization of system-level flourishing.

# Part I
The Premise

# 1
# The challenge

> "For much of the world, globalization as it has been managed seems like a pact with the devil."
>
> Joseph Stiglitz

In this chapter we identify the primary challenges that affect our socio-economic systems in their constant interaction with the natural environment and other living systems on the planet. They can be (artificially) separated as systemic and organizational challenges, since the interplay between the macro- and the micro-level actors at planetary scale is precisely what makes this a "wicked problem."[3] At the end of the chapter we will present a set of key ideas that encapsulate our approach to tackle the "wicked problem." They will be further detailed along with their conceptual, scientific, and managerial implications throughout the rest of the book.

## The systemic challenge

> "Perfection of means and confusion of goals seem in my opinion to characterize our age."
>
> Albert Einstein

Worldwide, July 2015 was the warmest month ever recorded. However, no one is impressed because such records are now broken with frightening frequency. The COP21 (Conference of the Parties) in Paris reminded us that the planet is already suffering from climate change and that conference-room resolve does not easily translate into action in the field. For example, the Arctic region is currently warming twice as fast as other areas; if the frozen organic matter in the permafrost soil thaws, the release of globally warming methane gas could accelerate the shrinking of polar ice caps with catastrophic consequences. As it is generally known, climate change manifests via extreme weather events, storms, and flooding, while also making drier areas drier, wiping out food supplies, and turning forests into kindling. Looking forward, we must anticipate tough times indeed. Sweeping adjustments are needed in such diverse areas as oil and mining industries, transport and energy, intensive agriculture, industrial production, and consumer behavior. The coping mechanism of corporations, which we recognize as key actors, will be a critical component of the collective response to these unprecedented systemic challenges.

On the social front, there are already sobering consequences associated with increasing social inequality within virtually all developed countries. According to recent Organisation for Economic Co-operation and Development (OECD) research,[4] the income ratio between the top and bottom 10% of wage earners in OECD countries has reached almost 10 on average (18.8 in the US), from 7.1 in the 1980s. Of course, technology has been favoring the concentration of wealth; however, when a global corporation reaches a worth of $700 billion, it raises questions that a traditional mindset is not equipped to address.

For the top 1%, the growth in share of the total income is even faster and the super-rich are often feeding the intricate offshore "fiscal optimization" industry. This global macro-economic crisis has made things even worse by significantly weakening the bottom 40% of the population in most countries. Interestingly, one of the consequences of this increasing gap between the rich and poor is that the poor and the squeezed middle-class families tend to underinvest in education, which can weaken nationwide recovery and ensuing levels of prosperity.

On the political front, the impact of these trends in democratic countries, where the average voter continues to pay taxes, undermines societal consensus and faith in politicians and institutions at large. Large political parties are losing out to dark-horse contenders and fringe groups of discontent voters with untested policies and opaque agendas. Thus, concerns about environmental sustainability and the unequal distribution of income are threatening not only the quality of life on the planet but also the likelihood (and magnitude) of economic growth in countries across the globe.

Needless to say, the two global maladies are tightly linked to each other in a vicious spiral. Climate change caused by environmental pollution will likely worsen the loss of soil fertility—due to drought, land degradation, and overuse of pesticides and chemicals. The negative impact on the environment will force increasingly larger populations to flee their native countries and search for a future in the most advanced economies. The International Panel on Climate Change (IPCC) projects that as many as 150 million individuals may be forced to flee their native coastal areas due to the rise in ocean levels. When we also consider economic migrants who are trying to escape lives of misery, the result is an ever-increasing social, environmental, and economic pressure on higher-income countries to find new models of development. Such development models would need to satisfy the interests not only of domestic actors (citizens, companies, etc.) but of players in a constantly broadening sphere of interconnected socio-economic-environmental systems.

Let us emphasize two points. Firstly, we need to realize that the challenge before us is to invest in both economic growth and environmental sustainability in an *integrated* way. It is both logically and ethically wrong to address each dimension of the challenge independently, given the tight interdependencies among the social, economic, and ecological systems. If we think about it for a moment, we would be hard-pressed to name one business decision of significance that has only economic consequences and no social ones. Almost every business decision will, at a minimum, affect a company's economic and social environment; many will also affect associated ecological systems.

Secondly, there is no single actor—whether the wealthiest country, the most powerful company or even cartel of companies—who can tackle the sustainability challenge alone. This "wicked problem" requires by definition a large-scale, cross-sector (public, private, civil), cross-disciplinary collaboration in order to begin to make sense of its complexity and identify, experiment with and diffuse possible solutions.

Still, there is some good news. The global engine that may stand a chance of addressing the sustainability challenge is finally starting to move, after many statements of vision and commitments and several "false starts" over the past couple of decades. After a long, multi-stakeholder process, at the 70th UN General Assembly of September 2015 the representatives of most countries of the world signed and committed to 17 Sustainable Development Goals (SDGs) broken down in approximately 170 specific sub-goals which capture the key areas of the sustainability problem.

The other major event in 2015 was the successful completion of a long-awaited agreement at the 21st COP in Paris that delineates the responsibilities of each country towards the stabilization of global climate change to capping temperature increases at no more than 2° Celsius above the average of the early '90s. This event is of historic proportions and not just for the sustainability agenda. However, we need to add that many keen observers of the climate change process are concerned by foreseeable loopholes in the necessary subsequent implementation of the Paris Agreement.

Of course, the signing of such agreements is one thing; however, the ability to ignite and significantly accelerate the speed of behavioral change at the individual or corporate level is quite another. The latter is a large-system-change challenge involving consumers, employees, investors, voters, and other stakeholders across sectors, value chains, and national boundaries.[5]

Thus, sustainability as commonly understood in terms of reduction of harm to environment and society is not sufficient. In order to ensure the lasting benefits of sustainability-as-flourishing we need a deep transformation of individual and organizational mindsets.[6] Otto Scharmer appropriately paraphrased Einstein's famous dictum: we cannot solve problems with the same consciousness that created them.

This is the essence of the proposal we qualify as *the evolutionary leap* to the level of individual and organizational consciousness that can generate flourishing socio-economic and ecological systems. Such a leap aims at attaining an individual and collective awareness of the systemic nature of any business context. At this level of consciousness, business decisions *spontaneously* (as a natural reflex) aim to positively enhance the state of the system in its economic, social, and ecological dimensions rather (vs. serving solely personal or organizational interests).

## The organizational challenge

Do individuals and organizations have sufficient willpower and capacities to assume the proactive role of enablers and eventually as champions of the solutions to the aforementioned systemic challenges? This is a complicated question.

One of the main reasons for the slow system-wide progress has to do with the difficulties encountered by policymakers and regulators in stimulating, facilitating, and imposing significant behavioral changes on business organizations. These challenges require the development of an integrative mindset (on the part of business leaders, managers, and employees) and a transition to conceiving the role of the business as a source of value creation for all contributors (employees, customers, suppliers, communities, and investors). The relative voice and power distributed to each of them might vary significantly across time, sector, and institutional context and among competitors within the same contexts; however, they are all taken into account in relevant decision-making contexts (where their interests are at stake). This is sometimes referred to as the "great transition": it links the challenge of shifting individual mindsets and values with the changes necessary at organizational levels, so that system-level changes can be enabled.

When companies are committed to this transition, they must attempt to ensure adequate returns (for invested capital) and quality-of-life enhancements for the citizens in their communities and final consumers of their products. Such challenges might revolve around the design and creation of innovative products to satisfy true customer needs (vs. needs imagined by product managers) without taxing the quality of the environment (via closed-loop logistics and circular-economy solutions). Of course, the needs of internal stakeholders are somewhat different. The challenge, here, is for organizations to meet the goals of staff members who have dedicated their own professional aspirations and talents to their long-term success; this is to be achieved by changing performance evaluations, incentives, and career management systems to reflect relevant sustainability goals and translate them into individual and collective targets.

**The flourishing individual.** "Individual flourishing" refers to a transformation in human awareness whereby we are able to perceive ourselves and others at a deeper level via the cultivation of *collective consciousness* (explained in Chapter 5) and fully manifest the inbuilt qualities that exist in a potential form in every human being.

In Chapters 4 and 5, we will further examine the principles and attitudes that underpin the concept of individual flourishing, which are all embedded within us in a more or less active state. Of course, an important dimension of this challenge is the development of a diffused leadership (enacted by employees at large rather than only top managers) which promotes via its actions the identity and values of a flourishing organization.

> Flourishing at the individual level: the development of aptitudes (or virtues) to the fullest potential and realization of a state of completeness in the way we perceive (and connect to) ourselves and the rest of the world.

**The flourishing organization.** A Copernican revolution in the way we think of (and act as members of) socio-economic systems requires much more than just an understanding of sustainability and of the conditions for our collective long-term survival. John Ehrenfeld (MIT) and

Andrew Hoffman (University of Michigan)—two of the thought leaders and early contributors to the nascent field of corporate sustainability—claim in their "frank conversation on sustainability" that the key to the systemic crisis we are living in lies in our capacity to "flourish"[7] as individuals first, which will then generate flourishing organizations and ecosystems.

> **Flourishing organization:** an organization whose members have reached a state of collective consciousness where decisions and actions are geared to nurture and realize the development of the fullest potential for all the actors in the socio-economic and natural system.

By "flourishing" they refer to the development of the well-known aptitudes or virtues, realizing a state of completeness in the way we perceive and connect to ourselves and the rest of the world. It is about being as wise as we can and caring as much as possible for others' wellbeing, achieving satisfaction while reducing the urge to have and consume, controlling the drive to appear and command. It is about Being rather than Having.[8] These are all ethical, laudable, personal development goals that could very well transform businesses and societies as we know them—if taken seriously and achieved by at least a qualified minority of people worldwide (e.g., citizens, managers, politicians).

The reason why this type of transformation is such a "wicked" problem, not only at a system level but also at the organizational one, is that it requires the individual members of the organization to radically rethink virtually everything they learned in business school and in their professional experience thus far. It requires a complete reset of the way we think about what a business is, its purpose, and the way it should be run—all deeply ingrained elements in anyone who has worked within a business organization for any amount of time.

Of course, the purpose of business is to maximize shareholder wealth; any other purpose is a distraction (at best) and a transfer of wealth (at worst) from shareholders to other stakeholders. Shareholders comprise the only class of stakeholders who can claim residual gains (as dividends) after all the others have been paid. Thus, as the logic goes, they are supposed to be considered the owners of an entire company (although the only aspect they own is a portion of its financial capital). Clearly, such economic consequences (e.g., profits and losses) are disjointed from the social consequences of business decisions (which are considered only through the prism of economic results).

These assumptions have been at the core of business education, taken for granted and largely acted upon by managers—albeit unconsciously. However, they are ethically and logically flawed and can impede the sustainable progress of socio-economic systems. Eminent law scholars[9] have credibly debunked the reductive assumptions related to the purpose of business, the primacy of shareholder interests, and the idea of unique access to residual claims from the outcome of company activity. In fact, even under the generally permissive corporate laws in the State of Delaware, the board of a corporation has to act in the long-term interest of the company first, and only afterwards of its shareholders. Employees, and any other stakeholders, can be invited to be part of the board and of any strategic committee, can be given access to the residuals from the business activity as a partial, or even total, form of compensation in recognition for their contributions to the success of the company. However, while profit is imperative for company survival, it is generally not the sole reason for its creation or existence.

## From challenge to solution

"Knowing others is intelligence; knowing yourself is true wisdom."

Lao Tzu

At a micro-organizational scale, the aforementioned "great transition" takes on a specific meaning, since it questions the very purpose of the business enterprise and types of mission that society expects it to pursue. Rapidly emerging models of the new business enterprise emphasize the goal of satisfying the interests of all the actors who contribute to the success of the enterprise, including capital investors, employees, customers, suppliers, and communities (the five so-called "core" stakeholders[10]).

Needless to say, a business enterprise will wish to develop a whole new way to operate when it has such goals—and a comprehensive perimeter that includes the interests and voices of all relevant actors. This "whole new way" is increasingly popular among entrepreneurs and startups across the world and often results in a so-called "hybrid" or "social" form of business. Indeed, thousands of businesses are now being created with integrated economic and social–environmental purposes that are clearly defined in their mission statements and organized in a stakeholder-oriented fashion.

But how can existing corporations evolve towards the defining characteristics of flourishing organizations? This is the heart of the issue addressed in this book. However, while this approach is still considered cutting-edge, we believe that (i) the most pressing dimensions of the problem are readily understood (especially at the macro-systemic level, based on the incontrovertible evidence brought by environmental and social scientists); (ii) overcoming the aforementioned systemic and organizational challenges is possible; and (iii) it is possible to start visualizing what a sustainable endgame might look like—even though opinions on details may differ substantially depending on political and cultural beliefs.

Business scholars and practitioners have been discussing what sustainability means for decades now. The ideas are converging around commonly discussed traits such as corporate responsibility and accountability, environmental sensitivity, social inclusion, stakeholder orientation, and so on.

However, what we don't know yet are the best ways to start the transformational engine and guide, to the extent possible, the evolution of organizations and systems towards the realization of those sustainability conditions. Possibly even less clear is how the "flourishing" conditions could be met. How can individuals work on the deepest dimensions of their self to strengthen capabilities (virtue) and reduce shortcomings (vice)—in sustainability terms? How can organizations and policymakers encourage, stimulate, and even guide these subtle evolutionary processes that may already be at work deep inside individuals—long before outward behavioral manifestations (consumption, saving, investment, work effort, business strategy, public policy, etc.) can be observed? Furthermore, can such qualities of human nature be significantly shaped and made subject to self-determined evolutionary processes?

This brings us to the core premise of the book. We believe that we have a sufficient amount of evidence, which we will share in the following chapters, to suggest that the following propositions are *plausible* and, most importantly, *testable* by businesses that are serious about undertaking this transformational journey and becoming "flourishing organizations."[11]

---

*Proposition 1: Individual flourishing.* Individuals can positively influence the natural evolution of the cognitive, emotional, moral, and identity dimensions of their being through deep introspective and meditative practices. The evolution of these individual traits can in turn influence the quality of business decisions and actions undertaken in organizations, from a long-term economic, social, and environmental sustainability perspective.

---

*Proposition 2: Organizational evolution.* *The diffusion of these sustainability-oriented decisions and actions by individuals and small groups can then be supported by strategic, operating, and cultural change[12] initiatives undertaken by the organization. This would generate a virtuous cycle of bottom-up and top-down stimuli and responses, resulting in profound change in the purpose, identity, and mission of the organization, towards the creation and expansion of the common good for all contributing stakeholders.*

*Proposition 3: System flourishing.* *A stakeholder-oriented enterprise evolves to be a flourishing organization when it actively participates in the progress of its socio-economic and ecological system. Such ecosystems can flourish by cross-sector collaboration in stimulating[13] individual members to undertake consciousness-development practices (per Proposition 1) and organizations to set up experimentation and transformation cycles (per Proposition 2).*

A relatively small number of corporations such as Mitsubishi and Toyota in Japan, Interface and Patagonia in the U.S., Unilever and Marks & Spencer in the UK, Olivetti (now Telecom Italia Group) in Italy, and others, have been experimenting with some of these "flourishing-oriented" interventions. At a system level, policies in Costa Rica or large multi-stakeholder change initiatives (e.g., the Marine Stewardship and the Forest Stewardship Councils) are classic examples of sustainability-oriented initiatives with some of the envisioned traits.

Still, we are not aware of any organization—let alone ecosystem—that has been able to transform itself in such a fundamental way (i.e., across multiple dimensions of the sustainability challenge) to become a fully fledged "flourishing entity." Although several companies (led by enlightened figures) have been working to address this challenge, the inner/soft dimensions have proven to be, by far, the hardest ones to crack. For the most part, today's managers have been taught to view their roles in ways that are simply at odds with the required mindsets within flourishing companies. Furthermore, mere recognition of the potentially positive, complex impact of a corporation on its stakeholders yields insufficient data on how managers should modify their daily activities. Thus, we simply do not see a way around controlled experimentation, evidence-based selection, and organization-wide diffusion (described in the aforementioned propositions).

Consider the fact that placing a compass inside a magnetic field will make it point in a certain direction, depending on the nature and shape of the field. When you move its blade with your finger, it will only have a temporary effect (upon letting go, it will revert back to its earlier orientation). Likewise, no matter what changes are implemented within an organization, it will be difficult for a company to prosper if its internal compass (i.e., the thinking of its members and leaders) points in a different direction. In fact, the internal compass will return the organization to its old behaviors and actions, which, over time, will override the anticipated benefits of such changes—unless the organization's magnetic field itself changes.

This book offers a collective reflection on how it might be possible to change the magnetic field of an organization so that its internal compass enduringly points to true North.

# 2
# The leap in the field

"It is not because things are difficult that we do not dare; it is because we do not dare that they are difficult."

Lucius Anaeus Seneca

In this chapter, we attempt to solve the challenge delineated in Chapter 1 via the utilization of specific experiences and change interventions; they were assessed with context-specific metrics to evaluate their impact on the quality of managerial decisions and behaviors. We will collate elements of real case situations to outline the iterative process leading towards the desired change. Of course, not every setting described will currently allow for the precision of measurement and experimental design of a rigorous scientific endeavor. Still, we feel they offer insights indicative of the impact of meditative practices on managers in their own organizations.

## Development of consciousness through meditation: learning steps

The progression from individual consciousness towards the state of "dissolving" into the collective unconscious was described in detail by Swiss psychologist C.G. Jung in his book *The Relations between*

*Ego and the Unconscious.*[14] Jung (pp. 122-124) described *self-realization* as the "goal of life" itself. He called the self as something "living and superior ... an unfathomable being." He wrote that *individuation* is the process of becoming the self, which leads to the "realization of the collective purpose of a human being" (p. 59).

Individuation is the opposite of individualization, which according to Jung (pp. 21-44) is nothing but an illusion created by the conscious mind or ego. The ego is responsible for putting on various masks to suppress the true self from coming through; it creates the mirage of being an individual and strives to sustain that awareness. The individual masks that create a "second-hand reality" are described by Jung as *personae*, which incidentally was the term used in the theatre of antiquity for the masks the actors wore to represent the character they enacted.

We can say that our *persona* consists of our ego and conditionings. The *persona* builds up false identifications in life such as names, positions, and titles, and tries to overlay the *collective unconscious* which dictates the game in reality. In this manner, the *persona* affects the individual unconscious through the variety of artificial options it offers.

The collective unconscious can be understood as something that, as opposed to the individual unconscious, goes beyond the limits of the individual due to its intrinsic collective nature. It represents inherited categories or *archetypes* and is thus much greater than the mere collective memory of humankind. The collective unconscious strives to reproduce the archetypes that come to us as pictures, figures, and aptitudes.

Thus, the *persona* lures us into the perception that something such as the *individual* has its own existence, while the process of *individuation* leads to the greater experience of the true self which mirrors the collective unconscious. After becoming the self, the awareness expands into collective consciousness. This inner transformation is akin to a drop that falls in the ocean, dissolves into it, and is aware that it has become the ocean. The approach we propose is by its nature holistic and controlled by the collective unconscious into which the experimenters are able to tap in the silence of meditation.

Shortly before his death in 1970, American psychologist Abraham Maslow added another level at the very top of his hierarchy of needs, deeming his own earlier view, which stopped at *self-actualization*, as too limiting. He named this last level *self-transcendence*.[15] He described it as the seeking of a dimension that lies beyond all systems we know as obvious or self-evident. Maslow's state of *transcendence* corresponds to Jung's state of *self-realization*.

In order to better understand and appreciate the case studies, we will provide here a brief background on a few key meditation concepts, which we will elaborate upon in subsequent chapters.

The state of *thoughtless awareness* (being aware, in the present moment, without thinking), which will be discussed in more depth in Chapter 3, is a key part of the foundation comprising our hypothesis. This state can be achieved through an innovative meditative technique which we will call *spontaneous meditation*. The name itself hints at the fact that the state of thoughtless awareness is reached not through effort, but rather through the spontaneous activation of an inner *catalytic energy*, described in Chapter 4. Although the awakening of this energy is not achieved through effort (which leads to mental tension and generates more thoughts rather than dissolving them), regular practice of this type of meditation over sustained periods of months and years is important as this is a process that takes time to master and unfold.

When activated, the catalytic energy rises through the spine starting from the sacrum bone. On its way up to the top of the head, it passes through seven *aptitude centers*, the qualities of which correspond loosely to Jung's archetypes. The catalytic energy purifies and nourishes the aptitude centers on an energetic level, bringing out their qualities and restoring physical, mental, and emotional balance. This energy is key to opening the door to the collective unconscious described by Jung, which then starts to become increasingly conscious to the practitioner. Practitioners gradually become *collectively conscious*, able to feel in a *tangible way* their own aptitude centers and the aptitude centers of others. Thus, they are able to perceive the fundamental nature of themselves and of others, in the form of "building blocks" represented by the aptitude centers in every human being. Importantly, this tangible perception is registered on the central nervous system on a par with how we directly experience what we feel with our five senses (i.e., with the same level of concreteness as seeing that the sky is blue or feeling that the fire is hot).

We invite the reader to accept the above as a hypothesis, which will be further developed in subsequent chapters. However, our observation is that, if there is genuine seeking for a dimension beyond the obvious, the effects of meditation can help individuals and organizations further their journey towards the flourishing state. Even if such seeking is not present at the outset, the sustained practice of spontaneous meditation widens the path of inner evolution every time the meditator enters the state of thoughtless awareness. This progression towards the individual flourishing state is enabled through the activation of the catalytic energy, which helps us feel the seven energetic aptitude centers as we shall see in Chapter 4. The outcome of these meditative processes is the strengthening of emotional stability and of the power of introspection; in their absence, it is difficult to see through the clouds of our *persona*.

We characterize this specific type of meditation based on thoughtless awareness as a process leading to a level of recognition of one's own true self (rather than replacing existing conditionings with other conditionings). In the state of thoughtless awareness, when the meditator is fully aware and alert but at the same time relaxed and without thought, negative feelings (anger, fear, jealousy, and other emotions that are not helpful for the resolution of our problems) fade away. This is by no means an escape; instead, it builds a link to the largest resource we can tap into for generating breakthrough solutions to the problems in our lives—the collective unconscious as described by Jung.

The journey towards flourishing begins where Maslow had left off (i.e., at the level of *transcendence*). There are, in fact, five hierarchic levels of learning, which should not be seen as static or discrete but as dynamic, overlapping states that build on one another. Figure 1 provides an overview of the five learning steps in the upper, inverted pyramid. Chapters 6 and 7 will further describe how to effectively make progress towards becoming a flourishing organization.

## Five learning steps in the field of collective consciousness

Individual flourishing begins with the first two levels: *Know Thyself* and *Master Thyself*. The third level of *Collective Consciousness* is where the effects on the individual start reaching out and blending into other individuals, and the bridge to collective flourishing is built. In Levels 4 and 5 the individual development is increasingly put into the service of the organization and then the system (other organizations and stakeholders, the environment, the world). Level 4 focuses on the flourishing of the organization itself; however, Level 5 breaks those boundaries as it reflects the identification with the good of the "whole" (i.e., the system).

> Individual growth is ultimately the factor that determines how quickly the organization will progress towards producing sustainable decisions and behaviors. The three lower levels in the upper pyramid build the critical base without which growth on the higher levels cannot happen. This is particularly important to mention, as extraordinary success can easily blur the sight of the foundation upon which it is built.

| Level 1 | Know Thyself | Individual flourishing starts with *self-realization* via the activation of the catalytic energy and spontaneous meditation based on thoughtless awareness (see Chapter 4). This constitutes a first step towards unmasking the "second-hand reality" of the *persona*. |
|---|---|---|
| Level 2 | Master Thyself | Misidentifications become apparent in the light of the new dimension of awareness achieved through meditation (cognitive change—see Chapters 4 and 5). Behavior, emotional traits, and values begin to change through the inner transformation process. |
| Level 3 | Collective Consciousness | Collective Consciousness allows us to reach the highest level of empathy through a deeper perception of ourselves and others, which is felt directly on the central nervous system (Chapter 5). The aptitude centers begin to increasingly manifest their respective archetypical qualities (Chapter 4) and they positively affect others. |

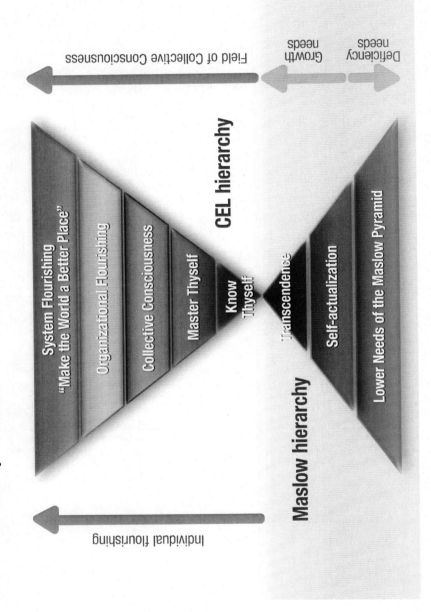

FIGURE 1. Evolutionary hierarchies

| Level 4 | Organization Flourishing | The flourishing individual engenders sustainability-oriented decisions, initiatives, and actions. They can then be supported by strategic, operating, and cultural change initiatives undertaken by the organization. This would generate a virtuous cycle of bottom-up and top-down stimuli and responses, resulting in profound transformations in the purpose, identity, and mission of the organization, towards the creation and expansion of the common good of all the stakeholders who contribute to it (see Chapters 1, 6, and 7). |
| --- | --- | --- |
| Level 5 | System Flourishing | As individuals become more socially responsible, they change their value system towards globally beneficial factors. The attitude shifts towards creating a stakeholder-oriented enterprise. It evolves towards a flourishing organization when it actively participates in the progress of its socio-economic and ecological system. Such ecosystems can flourish through cross-sector collaboration by stimulating individual members of the system to undertake consciousness development practices, and organizations to set up experimentation and transformation cycles towards globally sustainable solutions (see Chapter 1 and Conclusions). |

We cannot stress enough the fact that individual flourishing must be sustained throughout all levels, even when Level 5 is attained. Otherwise, everything will crumble like a house of cards. Thus, when individual development starts to be neglected and individuals go out of balance, at any level in the pyramid, the evolutionary movement deviates from its original path of holistic benevolence and shifts back towards an interest in individual gain (of a minority at the cost of the majority)—whether we are talking about an organization or the whole world.

> **Organizational flourishing is impossible without sustained individual flourishing throughout all phases of development.**

We will now proceed to explore some real-life case studies and research, in connection with each of the five levels, to generate a better understanding of the types of effects that can be expected from each step. This methodology can also be used as an evaluation tool throughout the training process.

## Level 1: Know Thyself

The initial steps of this experimental journey are towards knowing oneself at a profound level. As we have clarified earlier, and we will explain in more detail in subsequent chapters, such fundamental knowledge is attained via a new dimension of consciousness engendered by the activation of the catalytic energy. This new, deeper cognitive process goes beyond mental understanding and takes place in the silence of thoughtless awareness, where the self is experienced beyond the hustle and bustle of our ego, conditionings, and everyday thoughts. The building blocks of our being (i.e., the aptitude centers) are felt tangibly, on the central nervous system, and they provide us with information about ourselves at the deepest levels. In this state, meditators do not judge their actions and attitudes by "scripts" accumulated over a lifetime on the hard drive of the brain. Rather, they are able to view things relative to the inbuilt values of the aptitude centers, as explained in more detail in Chapters 4 and 5.

Think of the most arrogant person you know and recall the last time you tried to give them your feedback. Was the initiative fruitful? Did the person change and honestly see the point you were trying to make? Or did you end up with a headache, a useless discussion—or even a revenge situation? Such discussions usually do not work because the ego cannot see itself. Introspection—and the real growth of our consciousness—only start to occur after thoughtless awareness is experienced and gradually established. Although this requires regular practice, the resulting process of inner growth happens *spontaneously* (i.e., effortlessly).

The state of thoughtless awareness gives us a bird's eye view into our own true self; it is like a magic carpet that can take us to the space of the collective unconscious, where individuals and organizations begin their journey towards flourishing.

To illustrate this concept we will use a real-life example taken from a coaching session (names have been changed). Such one-on-one sessions are meant to trigger processes of self-knowledge and to lead towards the next step of self-mastery.

## Kathy: Mission impossible

Our coaching started long before our first formal session, at a dinner table in a seaside hotel. I was watching and listening to a highly competent young lady talk about things that, on the surface, made a lot of sense; however, I felt that, on the subtle level, her aptitude centers had certain blockages that bore the indications of depression. Guilt, sadness, and anxiety had, in fact, played a significant role in her situation.

I listened patiently to her business talk and then asked her why she felt so guilty. She was perplexed by the question and shocked by the reality it reflected. It was as if this released a wave of honesty in her and she immediately asked me to be her coach. I was able to get to this point in the conversation by using an aspect of Level 3 (collective consciousness) described in the above table, which allowed me to assess Kathy's issues at a fundamental level.

The first session consisted of Kathy accepting her problem and taking the first step towards Level 1: *Know Thyself*. She had been a victim of a "corporate mobbing"[16] incident and received a few coaching sessions provided by her company; however, this had done little to improve her situation. Coaching, in fact, frequently does not bring long-term, sustainable change. The reason for this is manifold, although it often has to do with the fact that a self-destructive cognitive, emotional, or behavioral pattern is simply replaced with a less self-destructive pattern. Thus, the leaking hole at the subtle level of the personality—and the tendency to fall prey to negative patterns—remains unchanged. Coaches must be able to read the subtle behind the obvious and catalyze a sustainable impact via a non-cognitive, introspective coaching approach (which includes training in case-specific, self-healing techniques).

Kathy's company assigned us just five sessions. Under normal circumstances and given her initial state, such a small number of sessions would have fallen under the category "mission impossible" for a sustainable change. At our first session, Kathy acted as if she was doing fine. She stated that things were "not so bad" during the first 50 minutes of the two-hour session. I was using a typical question-based technique to gently get to know her state. She was in a phase of massive denial, while at the same time becoming increasingly aware that she had built up a façade with a see-through ceiling.

At a certain point in the conversation, a certain trigger was pulled and she started crying. She had been suppressing a lot of tension for an entire month and it was now being released. Such moments can have an effect of great relief if guided properly; however, they can also cause a deeper depressive state if the negative emotions reinforce themselves. When Kathy was about to take a dive into the deeper realms of her feelings of helplessness, I felt it was the right time to activate her catalytic energy. I explained to her that we should try some energy work that might prove helpful.

As Kathy prepared for meditation and her catalytic energy became activated (using the collective consciousness provided by Level 3), I felt the left sympathetic nervous system (emotional side) heavily affected, as expected. There was also a blockage on an aptitude center that indicated a high level of guilt. I used the techniques of spontaneous meditation to bring these aspects into balance, and within a few minutes her crying subsided—until it stopped completely. As this balance was established, I helped her catalytic energy rise again.

She became absolutely silent, spontaneously fell into a deep meditation and sat without moving for quite some time, evidently enjoying the release she felt in that state. After about ten minutes, Kathy opened her eyes. They were sparkling, her pupils were dilated (indicating a state of relaxation), her face had regained color, her forehead was smooth, and she looked ten years younger—almost like a little girl. Her first words were: "Wow—I am in another universe!" I shared with her a few simple techniques for balancing herself in meditation and we parted ways. This marked Kathy's entrance into Level 1: *Know Thyself*.

I have witnessed the transformational power of the catalytic energy numerous times. Most importantly, it appears to work on the source of a (negative) emotion and thus heal it. For example, imagine erasing a negative entry on a hard drive by simply allowing the perfect image of the original drive to re-emerge; similarly, rather than supplanting pre-existing conditionings with new ones, Kathy's negative emotions seemed to have vanished into thin air. This is consistent with results that many long-term meditators have reported via our RESPONSE study (presented at the end of this chapter).

For our second session, we considered a variety of methods for handling Kathy's corporate mobbing scenario and brought her closer to the second level: *Master Thyself*. During the third session, we focused on the importance of planning and establishing timelines, and uncovered patterns that kept Kathy away from completing her doctoral degree. In the fourth session, we developed an action plan and Kathy signed a "contract" with herself.

This is what happened at a superficial level during our sessions. On a deeper level, we used approximately 25 minutes during each session to learn more about meditation and inner balancing—including 15 minutes of actual meditation practice. Kathy kept to her meditative practice at home and came back as a stronger personality each time we met.

During the fourth session, Kathy proudly shared with me her decision to go for an ex-pat job as a country manager, which her company had offered and which enabled her to complete her PhD thesis. This was something she would not have dared to even consider prior to starting our sessions. I was not sure that she would be ready for such an adventure so soon. She proved me wrong.

I met her two years later. She looked emotionally very stable, had completed her thesis, and had expanded her region from a rather insignificant chapter of her company to an important emerging market. She had reached the level of elevating her organization.

## Level 2: Master Thyself

### 2a. Global-scale wellbeing

Kathy's situation illustrated that knowing the self provides a foundation for initiating a journey towards individual flourishing; however, it takes a significant amount of work to get rid of bad habits and emotions. Negative emotions have a tendency to become "sticky"—particularly once they reinforce themselves. Thus it is extremely difficult, albeit very important, to break this vicious cycle. The following two case studies demonstrate how this can be accomplished on a global level.

Hewlett Packard is an enterprise with significant focus on sustainability as well as personal development, including wellness and stress management aspects. The company has its own internal Sustainability Network, which spans all continents and is composed of employees passionate about cultivating and promoting sustainable practices at work and at home. The HP Sustainability Network agreed to experiment with the use of meditation-based stress management techniques in order to a) increase employee wellbeing and productivity and reduce absenteeism, and b) encourage an increase in sustainability awareness and practice. The idea behind the second point was based on the fact that work stress causes a phenomenon known as "tunnel vision," where the stressed individual's focus is reduced to the immediate, self-relevant, narrowly perceived consequences. If stress is alleviated, the individual's sphere of interest and action enlarges to include a sustainable lifestyle and to experiment with new ideas and innovative work practices.

The pilot intervention was launched with an initial group of 26 employees. Programs consisted of 30-minute sessions held weekly, where typically the first 10 minutes were dedicated to the presentation of concepts and the subsequent 20 minutes were reserved for guided group meditations. Pre- and post-meditation questionnaires were distributed to participants at each session over 12 consecutive weeks. The questionnaire was a simplified version of the standardized General Health Questionnaire (GHQ-12), distilled down to five questions pertaining to the physical (fatigue) and psychological (sadness, anxiety, fear, nervousness, anger) state of the participants. At the end of the 12-week period, 96% of the participants indicated overall improvement.

Based on the results of the pilot, HP Human Resources recognized the value of the methodology and encouraged a greater employee participation at the Plano, Texas location, which resulted in a new series of programs attended by 70 participants. Word quickly spread as other HP Sustainability Network chapters found out about the success of the programs; after a few months, a new series of distance learning sessions was organized—with more than 700 employees from 14 countries signing up.

The sheer numerical expansion and feedback received left little doubt about the impact of this program on multiple business-relevant dimensions, going significantly beyond work stress reduction and psychological wellbeing. For instance, it was interesting to note that first-session feedback impressions consisted of one-liners, which after a few weeks became multiple sentences and after a few months became whole paragraphs. Clearly, a pleasant initial experience (occasionally dramatically positive and punctuated by several exclamation marks) evolved over time into significant changes that participants could perceive in themselves with increasing clarity. After an even longer period of time, this occasionally resulted in reports of life-altering, profound changes. For example, one employee told us that not only is she now a better worker but she is also a better mother; another HP employee felt a sense of clear guidance and inspiration in her work and attained significant improvements in her overall health and ability to sleep soundly every night—an issue that had plagued her for many years.

Similar results were obtained via other programs within the corporate offices of Walmart in California, where participants worked in pairs to assess each other's inner states in addition to their own. Employees were able to use their newly developed collective consciousness to help each other in progressing further on their journeys towards flourishing—going significantly beyond the initial goals of stress reduction and wellbeing.

## 2b. An "almost boring" exercise

A corporation in the natural resources sector set out to create a psychologically challenging training for their region's high-potential team members. The goal was for the participants to learn and experience mental strategies that could help them remain "on top of the situation" in difficult circumstances while improving their resilience to stress. One of the exercises of choice involved the use the "pamper pole" which is a pole of 10 meters (approximately 11 yards) in height with iron supports sticking out of its sides to facilitate climbing. At top of the pole a small plate was fixed with a diameter of about 30 centimeters (1 foot) on which standing would be comfortable. The climbers were secured through a rope above their heads by their teammates. Once the participants reached the top and stood up straight, the only way they could come down was to jump and rely on their teammates to hold on tight to the rope.

**FIGURE 2. Pole pamper teambuilding exercise**

This exercise poignantly depicted the manner in which problems are created by thought processes alone. While they were still in the safety of the conference room, participants were asked to step on a plate of the same size and balance themselves on it—a simple exercise. Later on, the participants walked outside and were again asked to balance themselves on the plate—this time 10 meters up, on the pole. They unpacked their climbing gear, and a number of dramatic and sometimes humorous scenes ensued.

Try to picture a participant who has reached the top of the pole and attempts to get their weight over the plate in order to stand on it. Often, the legs want to push the body up but the arms hold so tightly to the pole that the body remains fixed in the same place. This is a position where maximum effort is invested with zero resulting progress, leading soon to exhaustion without a chance of completing the exercise successfully. Evidently, the two cognitions are in conflict with each other and send opposite orders to the body; this aspect caused interesting debates in the debriefing phase.

The exercise described ordinarily exposes strengths and weaknesses in an emotional setting; however, its focus can vary according to the objectives of the workshop (there is typically a different approach for team development, personal development, leadership skills, or incentives). In this particular case, participants were given as much time as they needed until they were able to develop their own strategies for completing the task within a specified, short duration. The first half of the group simply climbed using strategies they had developed beforehand; however, out of the eight participants, three did not make it at all and the rest exceeded the allotted time by almost 200%. Subsequently, the whole group learned how to meditate; the participants went into a deep state of thoughtless awareness and then the second half of the group was released to climb. All of them were successful; in fact, they completed the exercise in less than 80% of their allotted time.

During the debriefing, the second group mentioned how easy it was for them to just see the task at hand, focus their attention, and then execute. They reported that it was very easy to remain cool during the crucial moments and simply follow through on their plans. Somebody commented: "It was just like climbing on a chair—very easy and *almost boring*!"

## 2c. Biofeedback measurements of instant stress reduction

Thus far, we have highlighted some aspects of mastery over negative emotions that concern mainly the individual whose nervous system is creating these emotions. As it turns out, particularly in the case of stress-related incidents, there exists a tendency to share negative emotions with others. For example, it is not uncommon for participants involved in—or even observing—an incident to feel negative emotions spreading even faster than positive ones. Anxiety, guilt, depression, and anger can all dissolve into a state of balance through meditation in thoughtless awareness.

A certain continuity of meditative attention and practice is necessary in order to attain sustainable results and inner mastery. Once the catalytic energy is activated, the path is cleared for attaining thoughtless awareness. This can be compared to learning to swim or to ride a bicycle. Once the learning "clicks" in the nervous system, you will always know how to do it, even after taking a break from it for many years. However, what does it take to become a champion? This, of course, requires intensive training, which is quite rewarding with meditation. In fact, it is almost impossible to describe the numerous moments of silent transformations that we have witnessed during our seminars and workshops.

Biofeedback devices have been occasionally used to monitor changes in stress-related parameters during meditation sessions. Skin conductance (SC)[17] is one such parameter that is very easy to measure, reacts very quickly to virtually the smallest stimulus, and indicates increased tension when it is elevated (and relaxation when it is low). Interestingly, after an increase in SC (via stress), it normally takes some time for it to come back down to a normal level. After several weeks of biofeedback training, however, it may be possible to reduce the value of SC substantially within a reasonable amount of time.

Figure 3 presents a graph of SC values that were captured at a workshop attended by a group of managers from a global logistics corporation at a mountain retreat in Austria. The subject was chosen on a voluntary basis; the rest of the group would watch his progress on the screen. This aspect, alone, could be considered as a somewhat stressful factor for the subject (who had no history of relaxation training and was connected to an electrode capable of measuring skin conductance).

From start to about 2½ minutes into the experience, the subject became slightly stressed, likely due to his exposure to the rest of the group. However, after 2½ minutes the subject was asked to relax, which produced a small improvement. Four minutes later, meditation was introduced to the subject. Interestingly, the SC not only dropped significantly but the variation of the subject's SC also decreased. The graph became smoother, which indicated a process of inner stabilization. After another minute, the graph crossed the baseline value of 2.3 and dropped down to 1.5 at the end of the exercise. Remarkably, this tangible reduction in stress happened with about 20 colleagues looking on (and the subject being aware of it).

**FIGURE 3.** Drop in skin conductance after meditation

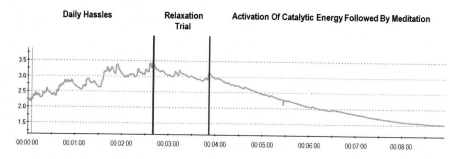

Figure 4 shows the result in a different setting. A group of about 20 members of the Women in Leadership group met in Brussels, Belgium for an EU-sponsored platform meeting. The topic of meditation was introduced, after which a group meditation was led while using a biofeedback device to measure the progress of inner silence. A female volunteer from the audience was attached to the electrode during meditation; however, on this occasion all participants were also asked to follow the same meditation instructions simultaneously. The entire audience was able to experience deep inner peace, which was also reflected on the graph of the volunteer (whose SC was measured).

A very significant drop of the SC plateaued at the level of 0.5, which is, objectively speaking, an extremely low value and indicative of a deep state of relaxation. This was illustrative of the power of collective consciousness, specifically when meditation is practiced in a group.

**FIGURE 4.** Drop in skin conductance: second measurement

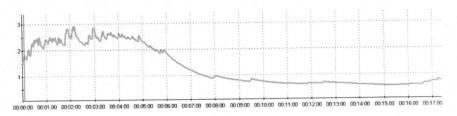

## Level 3: Becoming collectively aware—empathy and beyond

### 3a. Making a joint venture work: the bird's eye view

Mahatma Gandhi, the acclaimed leader of a nation of 1 billion people, had included in his daily prayer a famous Hindi song from the 15th century, *Vaishnava Jana To*. In its first verse, the song says that those who have become their true self can feel the pain of others. Ever since Daniel Goleman wrote his seminal book on emotional intelligence, it has become widely acknowledged that empathy is a key area of competence in many aspects of life—particularly for business leaders. Goleman defines empathy as "to know what others feel."[18] Once we know ourselves and are able to master ourselves, we need to learn how to develop genuine empathy.

According to Goleman, who in turn quotes Stern, genuine empathy builds during early childhood in the rapport between mother and child and requires a frequent fine-tuning of eye contact between the two. Needless to say, it does not provide a good perspective if for whatever reason that rapport does not take place the way it should in one's own childhood. Spontaneous meditation is a very quick-acting method for internalizing empathy through the activation of the aptitude center responsible for it (more details in Chapter 4). A sense of increased, objective self-awareness is also a helpful resource for improving empathy.

Empathy enables us to read and correctly understand the subtle signals of spoken and body language and mimic resonance and many other messages that are sent during intended (and unintended) communication processes. We can often lose ourselves completely into conversations and forego the dignity of the "bigger picture" that allows us to remain on top of a situation. In such moments, feelings can be hurt and negotiations can collapse; it can take years for such wounds to heal.

Through the experimental journey we described, we found that we are able to touch the realm of collective consciousness, which reaches to a level that is even deeper than empathy. Collective consciousness allows us to feel our own aptitude centers, as well as those of others, and shows us how deeply our connection to the self has grown—and how wide the door to collective consciousness has opened. However, it remains unused for much of the time.

This level of consciousness is perhaps the most experimental one, as this new awareness, though fully "uploaded and installed," needs to be discovered through daily application. To use an analogy: at this stage, the ability to remain in the bird's eye view, to see the full picture from above, is actually fully established but is only practiced in exceptional moments.

At the outset of our workshops, we have found ourselves confronted on many occasions with highly complex situations, such as hatred, distrust and jealousy among colleagues, or

> Like a city-hopper airplane, the aspirant takes off and enjoys the brief sojourn in the sky, perhaps interrupted by turbulence, which is followed immediately by the airplane's descent and landing back onto the ground. Then the scene repeats itself after some time. There is a great experience up in the clouds, but it is of a short duration and any distraction brings the plane soon back on the ground.
>
> Through the empiric deepening of the meditative state, the meditator's awareness gets elevated to collective consciousness (to be described in detail in Chapter 5). Then, the practitioner is no longer a city-hopper but becomes a first-class transatlantic flyer who goes the distance needed to really flourish and to help their organization and the world to progress on their path towards flourishing.

hidden feelings and agendas between managers and team members with long histories of mutual emotional injuries. (Needless to say, all such factors acted as towering stumbling blocks in the way of the organization's progress.) We customized our methods and dramaturgy to each specific situation and noticed that the ride became a rollercoaster when we worked with methods based on cognitive solutions; however, the circumstances dramatically changed as soon as we brought in the spontaneous meditation technique. Like a flying carpet, meditation took individuals above the landscapes of their daily episodes, constraints, and problems.

A €4 billion international joint venture project in an eastern European country ran into a communications gridlock due to (i) interpersonal conflicts that had spiraled out of control over the course of an emotionally charged year and (ii) parent companies (of the joint venture) that were displaying their own agendas and in defiance of regional parties associated with the management board. This was making a fruitful collaboration virtually impossible. Differing views were collected from the main actors, followed by a workshop where different cognitive methods were attempted for getting the opposing parties to open up; however, there was hardly any progress registered, due to two key factors:

*An inability to have empathy for the problems of others.* As participants were stressed due to their situation (which they assumed was caused solely by the other party), they did not exhibit the slightest interest in having empathy.

*An inability to see the situation from a meta-level* (i.e., the "magic carpet" or "bird's-eye" view), which would have enabled them to focus on the common goal (vs. shortcomings of the other party).

The agenda was then changed to a non-cognitive, introspective type of intervention. If you cannot solve a problem, go beyond it!

There was no particular expectation that the parties in conflict would open up; nevertheless, everyone was invited to go into an experience of collective meditation. Before proceeding with the guided meditation, the pent-up energy in the participants was diverted into a competitive and demanding exercise which exhausted their physical energy while appearing to be an easy task. The pattern

## 2 THE LEAP IN THE FIELD    41

of tension was quickly broken as they sat back on their chairs. (An entirely new seating arrangement provided a change in visual—and thus mental—perspective.) Now participants were ready to jump into the state of meditation.

A guided meditation brought them into a beautiful state of inner silence where they attained a bird's-eye view of their situation and experienced their innermost being—the Self—which does not act but rather is in a witnessing state. In that state of thoughtless awareness, their individual consciousness merged into the collective consciousness and became a passive observer of external events—like a spectator watching a show.

> This is the moment when meditators begin to (i) observe their own actions from a holistic perspective, (ii) see the whole picture (stretched out like a map in front of them), and (iii) minimize identification with the "I" or ego as the vision of the whole increases. During these moments of deep inner silence, meditators transcend the motives of their behavior in favor of a wider reality. Through this spontaneous, effortless introspection and acquired self-knowledge, they are able to internally generate the resources needed for genuine changes in behavior.

After the exercise, an entirely different landscape emerged. The path was paved to find solutions to every item on our agenda. That evening, everyone signed approximately ten pages of mutual agreements on strategies and procedures, and even sang to the accompaniment of a guitar played by the trainer. Neither participants nor trainers had expected to attain such a level of team homogeneity—let alone achieving it within eight hours from the start of the workshop.

We realize the strength of a solution once it is tested. The following morning, the group got into a discussion that threatened to nullify all of the gains from the prior evening. Participants were asked to perform an exercise that plays around with association, dissociation, and meta-level notions beyond everyday life. The opposing parties were asked to (i) continue their discussion, (ii) formulate their own point of view, (iii) switch chairs, and (iv) consider the situation from the perspective of their counterpart—acting as the other person. This exercise is usually difficult to perform, as participants have a tendency to step out of their empathic dissociated states of mind under such circumstances.

After a short meditation break, the exercise worked flawlessly; participants showed a good ability to communicate other points of view, genuinely understood the associated motives, and produced a conclusion very rapidly. They were ultimately asked to consider their proposed solutions objectively and with a bird's-eye perspective. Once again, it took a few minutes of thoughtless awareness to enable the participants to properly identify with their roles; however, it was all smooth sailing afterwards. In fact, participants were astonished to have truly understood the positions of the other managers in such a clear way and with such a positive outcome. The entire group left the seminar venue in high spirits and earlier than planned because their job was done.

We found this episode to be significant as it illustrated the relationship established through meditation between selfhood and collective consciousness, which will be further explored in the following chapters.

## Level 4: Help the organization flourish

In retrospect, this meeting yielded not only improved mutual understanding but also charted a path for smoother organizational development. This was key as the joint venture was on the brink of destruction before the meeting; a lot of effort, resources, and good intentions stood on the verge of being wasted. This case study illustrated that the benefit of this experimental method (for organizational improvement) is dependent on integrative awareness, which is generated by the meditative state and ultimately challenges the manager in daily decision-making processes related to meetings, recruiting, conversing with employees, negotiations, and so on.

Above all, this process opens the path to *serendipity*, which enables the right things to occur at the right time and in the right place, without planning. Serendipity opens the horizon to innovation via intuition and paves the path towards conscious perception. However, it typically takes some time to learn how to listen to the whispering voice of intuition—especially after being used to working through endless lists of criteria and viewpoints in order to arrive at a conclusion.

An evolutionary leap at the organizational level requires either the support of a few key organizational players who have achieved a stable elevated level of awareness and are thus deeply grounded in the collective consciousness (i.e., a top-down approach), or alternatively a critical number of stakeholders who genuinely maintain and develop their basic level of meditative experience (i.e., a bottom-up approach). Naturally, the best results would occur in organizations that have a critical number of stakeholders who are all deeply rooted in meditation.

In Chapters 6 and 7 we shall introduce possible roadmaps for achieving flourishing organizations; however, we will now present two cases that focus on organizational development.

## 4a: The focus of attention

A global natural resources company in the Middle East, whose negotiations sometimes involved billion-dollar deals, was faced with the challenge of staying focused during cross-cultural, long-term negotiations with multiple parties at the same table. The HR team aimed to improve the attention span of managers and employees and develop a greater ability to take on risks. At the beginning and end of a six-week intervention, the attention spans of participants was tested using one of the best attention performance tests on the market: the D2 test.[19] No participant had a lesser score in the post-condition (vs. pre-measurement), with almost all participants exceeding their initial performance.

**FIGURE 5.** Significant increase in D2 measurements (attention performance) after meditation

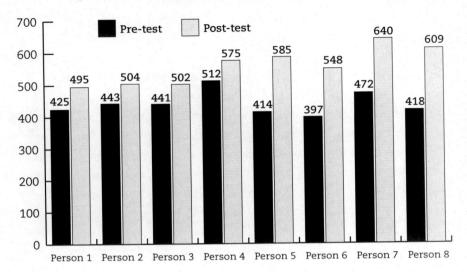

The comparison of the mean values showed that total concentration increased by far more than 100 points in the post-intervention measurement.

**FIGURE 6.** Overall D2 scores pre- and post-meditation

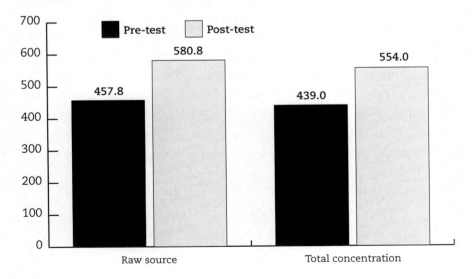

The above appeared to be a good score; however, it did not show how it would be ranked in comparison with other individuals. As the test was normalized, one possibility that emerged was to calculate the percentile ranks of the scores (e.g., a percentile rank of 83% indicated that 83% of the population achieved a lower score and 17% a higher one).

**FIGURE 7.** Concentration percentile scores pre- and post-meditation

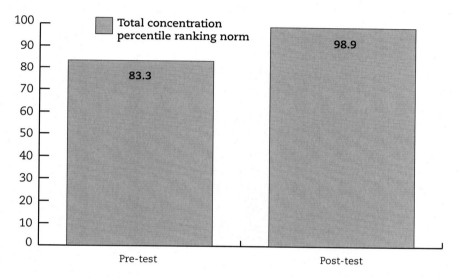

Although an improvement in attention test scores was the primary objective, participants were also asked to assess their own personal values and emotional traits through standard research questionnaires,[20] as well as providing answers to specific decision scenarios with sustainability trade-offs. The outcome was a clear shift towards socially conscious responses and towards caring for long-term consequences in decision scenarios. The results, associated with personal values, showed an interesting profile after six weeks of meditation based on thoughtless awareness.[21]

In a nutshell, the data indicates the development of managerial mindsets towards an increased ambition to succeed, and at the same time with a stronger drive for inner harmony. Furthermore, the pre-/post-meditation training assessments showed that self-control and emotional intelligence were given greater emphasis (compared to IQ) as guiding life principles. Overall, these shifts in personal values indicate that meditative practices influence not only the purely cognitive elements of our psychology, such as our ability to manage our attention, but also have profound effects on our emotional sphere and value systems. They promote evolutionary changes towards a more integrative view of success and, ultimately, of purpose.

## 4b: From individual to organizational advantage

Unfortunately, the effects of training and coaching interventions are generally short-lived and poorly measured. In the vast majority of cases, the only measured outcome is the satisfaction of participants associated with the intervention (vs. any actual impacts on individual and organizational practices). However, this does not need to be the case if requisite care is taken, in advance, to select and assess appropriate impact evaluation procedures and measures.

A relatively small electronics retailer with approximately 250 employees and three outlets had successfully taken on the giants of the retail electronics market in Vienna, and was seeking to become number one in customer service in their market segment. A training program was designed to coach all corporate employees from top management down to sales and reception via a sequence of workshops that included group meditation sessions among a variety of topics. Only a few participants repeated their meditation practices at home, in order to improve the sustainability of their meditative state.

Employees had the assigned objective of becoming industry leaders in customer service within one year. Once the training sessions were under way, 100 customers were randomly selected from the database and interviewed each month. The interviews were soon expanded to include six competitors, which represented the big players in the German-speaking market. Each interview lasted approximately 10–15 minutes. At the end of the entire period, we had gone through 2,150 interviews. At the conclusion of each interview, customers were asked to evaluate if they were *enthusiastic, satisfied, rather not satisfied*, or *absolutely not satisfied* with their latest shopping experience.

Figure 8 shows the development of customer satisfaction subsequent to the start of meditation training in June 2003, with June as a baseline. The graph shows a relatively steady increase in enthusiastic customers from month to month, rising to approximately 80%. Top-ranking keywords during the interviews were "feel good," "pleasant atmosphere," and "relaxed atmosphere." This seems to indicate that the practice of spontaneous meditation based on thoughtless awareness changes the emotional traits of practitioners; this transformation affects in turn everyone around them. In other words, the positive cycle between the individual and collective consciousness development appears to promote improvements in the emotional states of stakeholders, both internal and external to the organization.

**FIGURE 8.** Evolution of customer satisfaction scores over six months

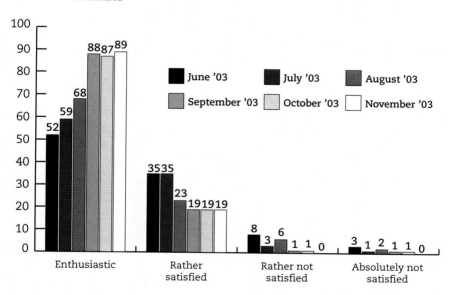

Earlier we mentioned that the 2,150 interviews were expanded to include competitors. Figure 9 is the result of a year-long study. The column on the right under "Enthusiastic" shows the mean value of customer satisfaction at a level of 77% for the above-mentioned electronics retailer. Also, it is interesting to note that the three competitors who showed the lowest percentages of enthusiastic customers are not in business anymore (and thus over 2,000 workers lost their jobs). These empirical findings were further validated by additional research (specifically, by IMAS) that confirmed these same trends.

**FIGURE 9.** Second study of customer satisfaction evolution

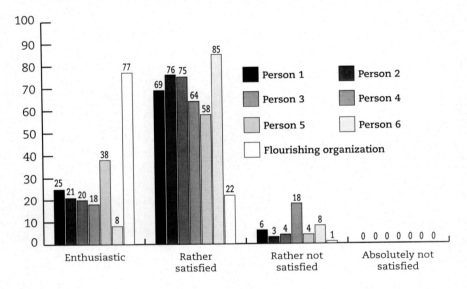

Of course, this story only provides a glimpse of the extraordinary possibilities that could be achieved if meditation, based on thoughtless awareness, were to be scaled up. By "scaling up," we are referring to the structured application of the initiative on an ongoing daily basis throughout an organization.

## Level 5: System Flourishing

Black holes, in our vast universe, are invisible. Skeptics could claim that they do not exist; however, astrophysicists accept their existence due to the attractive forces they generate. In a similar manner, the spontaneous manifestation of our dormant aptitudes suggests that there is something invisible, yet powerful, behind this phenomenon. Specifically, it reveals a change in the magnetic field of a personality (or organization) with positive effects at a systemic level.

When the collective consciousness starts to manifest in a persistent way within individuals, a wide set of related resources becomes available to them to draw upon. The extent of inner growth—into the sphere of thoughtless awareness—correlates to the benefits one can derive from it. Furthermore, in thoughtless awareness, the identification with the ego is reduced (akin to a drop dissolving into the ocean) via the identification with the true self which acts as a mirror of the whole. These notions will be rendered in detail in Chapters 4 and 5.

We submit the following hypothesis: the identification of the individual with the whole grows concurrently with the identification with global affairs (as practitioners progressively identify with their true selves). If this hypothesis proves true, one consequence is that experimenters of spontaneous meditation (i) become more socially responsible, (ii) adjust their value systems towards globally beneficial factors, and (iii) shift their managerial decisions towards higher outcomes (e.g., sustainable solutions).

Let us see if this hypothesis can be tested.

## 5a. RESPONSE project

What is the impact of meditation on sustainable decision-making in business?

For its Sixth Framework Program for Science, Technology Development and Application, the European Union focused on the strengthening the industry, its scientific basis, and its level of competitiveness. Within this program, the RESPONSE study was funded with €1,100,000 to create what for many years was the world's most comprehensive study on CSR. RESPONSE examined the gap between managers' and stakeholders' view about the role of business organizations in society, and identified factors that explain why the gap is larger in some companies than in others.[22] It did so in many ways, leveraging the insights from 450 interviews from a balanced sample of managers and stakeholders in 20 very large multinational companies (household names, such as IBM; Microsoft and J&J from the U.S.; Unilever; Philips, Shell, and Heineken in the Netherlands; as well as many more European and global companies in the pharma, banking, electric energy, specialty chemicals, and mining sectors). To date, this project has generated six scientific articles published in top management journals (including the *Academy of Management Journal*, *Strategic Management Journal*, and the *Journal of International Business Studies*), in addition to a major report for the European Commission and several smaller managerial publications.

In four of the participant companies, RESPONSE also ran field experiments to tackle the complex question of how the perception gaps between managers and stakeholders can be reduced through several alternative forms of learning interventions. Overall, 93 managers participated in this portion of the research program, which juxtaposed standard executive education approaches to CSR training with non-standard methodologies based on meditative practices. The randomized experiments also controlled for "placebo" effects using relaxation (Hatha yoga) classes that held at the surface some similarities to the meditation methods but were not expected to produce consciousness development effects.

A battery of tests, including emotional traits (PANAS), psychological wellbeing (STAI), personal values (Schwartz), organizational culture perceptions (Inglehart), as well as decision scenarios with sustainability trade-offs and motivations for the decisions made, were used to assess the impact (pre/post differences) consequent to different learning interventions or control (placebo or no intervention).[23]

The first result that was remarkable through its "absence" was that the standard executive education approach, with case discussions and lecturing, was ineffective in influencing the nature of decisions made by participant managers. In contrast, managers who went through meditation training significantly changed the nature of their decision-making, increasing the likelihood of choosing more environmentally and socially conscious alternatives *vis-à-vis* those that maximize short-term profit. Even managers in the "placebo" group with a relaxation training intervention showed to a certain degree trends in the direction of higher social and environmental consciousness, although much less accentuated than in the meditation training groups.

The most surprising aspect was that in both meditation and relaxation training there was no discussion of knowledge related to CSR or corporate sustainability. Participants only learned how to meditate or (for the active control group) how to perform yoga exercises. Furthermore, one should note that all the learning interventions were relatively time-contained, totaling nine contact hours over a six-week period. Yet their decision-making patterns, which were similar to their colleagues who were randomly selected to be part of the standard executive education class, changed in a statistically significant way towards more sustainable solutions.

What is the reason for this? The data we examined[24] points to three coherent sources of explanation. The first has to do with changes in the way managers evaluated the same type of decisions, after they went through the meditation training. The cognitive reasoning that determines the logic for business decision-making changed in the direction of higher sensitivity towards the social and environmental impact of those decisions. In addition, rationales that appeal to emotional factors, such as "because it shows compassion and caring" significantly increased in salience as drivers of business decisions, whereas reputation and short-term profitability became considerably less relevant when compared to pre-training levels.

The second source of explanation revealed by the analyzed data is related to changes in the emotional traits. These traits are not temporary moods, but stable emotional states that characterize each of us, and are eventually subject only to rare, slow (and typically unconscious) change. Participant managers were asked to complete a standardized psychological scale to rate their emotional state ("to what extent have you felt this way over the last four weeks?") across a comprehensive list of positive and negative emotions. Statistical comparisons between the pre- and post-training answers showed a significant increase in their positive emotional traits such as "happiness" and "courage," as well as "feeling inspired" (although with a slightly lower level of statistical significance).[25] Moreover, the negative emotional states (such as "sadness," "anger," "feeling tired," and "nervousness") of managers in the meditation group significantly decreased after the practice of meditation.

The third source of explanation was perhaps the most surprising, given the limited length of the training program: the data shows significant changes in the value system of members of meditation groups. For instance, "unity with nature," "a world of beauty," and "forgiving" (as guiding principles for one's life) all significantly increased in their importance among the meditation group with respect to their baseline levels. Also, the importance of "preserve my public image" significantly decreased from the pre-training levels. Finally, the salience of "wisdom," "inner harmony," and "responsibility" increased in the meditation group, although at slightly lower levels of statistical significance when compared to the other traits.

These three sources of explanation had been associated in the scientific literature[26] with a view of sustainability that goes beyond the "do no harm" logic and focuses more on the "do good," consistently with the sustainability-as-flourishing approach we have taken in this book. However, the results of these experiments show that this mindset is not fixed or immutable. It is not just part of the identity of individuals, who can be (at best) selected on this basis for leadership positions in companies that are serious about transitioning to sustainability—rather, these personal traits and the sustainability-as-flourishing decision-making derived from them can, in fact, be learned. Moreover, the learning can happen in a relatively short amount of time, and without excessive investments on the part of the organization.

The only condition for this to happen, as it appears from the case studies and experiments reported above, is for the corporations to be willing to experiment with the introduction of innovative approaches to the management/leadership development challenges that they face in the sustainability transition process. Meditation, as thoughtless awareness, appears to produce deep personal development patterns that touch on all the relevant parts of our mindset that are involved in generating sustainable decisions and actions contributing to the flourishing of organizations and of the socio-ecological communities around them.

In the next chapter we will go more in depth to understand the neuroscientific bases of this statement that holds great promise for our sustainable development.

# Part II
# Individual Flourishing

# 3
# The neuroscientific evidence

> "Neuroscience will undoubtedly change out of all recognition a host of orthodoxies beloved in philosophy."
>
> **P.S. Churchland**[27]

Is it actually possible for us to utilize studied forms of introspection and meditation to develop mindsets associated with sustainability-as-flourishing? Is there scientific evidence supporting this? We believe so. In this chapter, we will discuss the scientific foundations supporting this proposition.

## What is meditation?

> "Life moves far more rapidly than it ever did before. What we need is a different type of human being."
>
> **Abraham Maslow**[28]

Truths and facts certainly seem to carry less weight in today's postmodernist world; however, business executives and others dealing with real-world issues cannot afford to cast them aside. Over the past 30 years, neuroscience research has auspiciously begun to provide answers to questions in the coveted domain of epistemology. How do we understand ourselves in relation to the world we live in? How do we know what we know? Could we ever really know the truth? Or are we strictly limited to perceiving the world via the tainted glass of our egos and conditionings? And, more importantly, can we improve our capacities to learn about ourselves, our roles, and our responsibilities *vis-à-vis* our multiple social contexts?

Of course, these fundamental questions have been debated over the history of humanity and many potential answers have been studied, tried, and refined. One major category of answers comes under a host of names (e.g., introspection, contemplation, meditation, mindfulness) and there have been other related concepts developed by various spiritual and cultural traditions across the globe. What has dramatically changed the landscape over the past two decades is the fact that scholars, across several disciplines, have started to conduct rigorous scientific research on the physiological, therapeutic, and behavioral consequences of many of these practices.

Before we examine relevant insights from these scientific efforts, let us first address key differences between these practices—and, in particular, the distinctive features of the deepest form of personal development and inner inquiry: meditation. How do we understand meditation? Is it a cultural inheritance? Folklore from the Far East? A tool to manage (and reduce) modern-day stress? A practice designed for certain spiritually oriented individuals to deepen their worship practices? Or a process to promote deeper (and broader) levels of consciousness and thus support our natural drive for self-improvement (and thus the betterment of society)? And, most importantly, is it a personal development process that is easily accessible to everyone—or just the few willing to prioritize it over all other aspects of life?

Westerners often consider meditation to be a form of concentration (i.e., an increased intensity of mental powers and a sort of condensed "mindful" thinking process). The concept of mindfulness has been particularly well received in Western countries over the past decade and is characterized by enhanced mental activity. This, of course, is necessary for bringing the attention inward and focusing on the breathing process—or outward, in a detached witnessing state. From a methodological point of view, these are considered key steps for training the attention towards the overarching objective of reaching a meditative state. Mindfulness can thus be viewed, more precisely, as a set of preliminary exercises for the attention—just as the practice of Hatha yoga was developed as a preliminary exercise for making the body accustomed to stillness. However, such practices encounter their own limits.

Certain types of meditation have been associated with hard-to-achieve benefits and unwanted side effects; however, if we explore the notion of meditation in Eastern cultures (particularly in India and China), we find that meditation is pursued as a daily discipline to optimize an individual's potential and the higher goal of *self-realization*. We can further describe the relationship between meditation and yoga via a simple image: meditation is the path and yoga is the destination. In fact, the word *yoga*, in Sanskrit, means "union." Meditation is the condition that allows the mind to experience a state of inner union with the higher aspects of our Self.

In other words, meditation is the way we realize the flourishing of our inner potential and become the best version of ourselves. Thus, while in some countries, meditation has been reduced to mere physical exercises (*asanas*), in others it is part of both ancient and everyday cultures. Interestingly, some widespread trends are emerging (e.g., India now has a Ministry of Yoga and the United Nations has accepted the 21st of June as International Yoga Day). In recent years, meditation has often been referred to as a practice leading to mindfulness or mental silence. However, our own experience shows that more can be accomplished.

The process of relaxing and breathing (*pranayama*) is useful but of lesser importance compared to internalizing our attention, letting the energy flow within us, and reaching a state of inner peace where we are able to experience a deeper perception of our being. Indeed, the state of wellness associated with this perception is beyond simple mental silence. This enjoyable state manifests in the absence of thoughts (thoughtless awareness, *Nirvichara Samadhi*) and brings a deep relaxation, but also, more importantly, an expanded and enhanced level of consciousness. In this specific state, we are closer to the realm of inspiration; we can more easily experience intuitions or insights that spontaneously surge from what Jung called the collective unconscious.[29] He declared that in his "line of research important parallels with yoga have come to light . . . These forms of yoga with their rich symbolism afford me invaluable comparative material for interpreting the collective unconscious . . . I . . . regard this spiritual achievement of the East as one of the greatest things the human mind has ever created."[30] This is the state in which we can begin to feel wonderfully well but also where creativity is enriched: we reach for the hidden, the new, for leading ideas and inspiration.

For the remainder of this book, we will refer to meditation as a specific state of expanded awareness that is devoid of thoughts; however, it is not attained via mental concentration. Beyond mindfulness, this condition of "thoughtless awareness" (being fully aware but without thinking) settles the attention in the present moment with no thoughts about the past or future. The present is where the individual experiences a brief period of inner silence, which can be lengthened with practice and enables a perception of the outer world that is much more intuitive, direct, and clear.

In the West, we often contrast action and contemplation. The concept of contemplation is actually closer to the genuine Eastern tradition of meditation. It is a state of silent witnessing of the inner environment which unveils insights about its object. It enhances our capacity to watch in a detached way and draw inspiration from a meta-cognitive state that enables us to see ourselves from an external viewer's perspective. This subtle, new-found knowledge represents an important step towards the overarching goal of self-realization.

> **Thoughtless awareness:** an elevated state of consciousness, characterized by the absence of thoughts coupled with a heightened faculty of perception.

Thoughtless awareness thus enables the deeper transformational power of the inner union (yoga) and sought-after harmony between action and contemplation. This unique state of being corresponds to the notion of meditation, as defined by the millennial traditions of Eastern cultures.

According to medical science, meditation is a *physiological* state of consciousness and as such has specific biological purposes. It has been argued that there are four physiological states of consciousness: sleeping, dreaming, "awake thinking" consciousness, and the meditative state. Each state or condition is associated with specific capacities and is necessary to perform different tasks. For example, we need to be "awake thinking" to drive a car, or listen to a lesson and store the associated information, while we need to be asleep in order to rest the body and allow melatonin to do its work on our immune systems.

Each state allows us to reach specific conditions, perform various tasks, and thus develop specific skills. This is akin to needing to go from a Desktop to Documents folder (in Microsoft Windows) in order to find a previously stored article. Although the computer is on and fully operational, we can only achieve these results if we go into the specific area of our computer that contains the data we need. Also, we can only access data from the web if our computer is connected to the network. The same computer can be used in entirely different ways depending on whether or not it can link with the rest of the world via the internet. Thus, two computers could look identical and have the same potential capabilities; however, one will be endowed with infinitely superior qualities via its connection to the internet (and ability to obtain key pieces of knowledge within a universe of data and other information). In a manner of speaking, this computer has "flourished" to its full potential.

A plausible definition of meditation is that it is a hypometabolic state (different from sleep) that promotes a physical, emotional, and mental relaxation and thus introduces an expanded consciousness and a new-found wellbeing.[31] As we will see shortly, this relates strongly to the concept of neuroplasticity. Scientists emphasize that the key difference between meditation and sleep is the heightened state of the attention. The topic of our attention is a highly important one; in any endeavor, our success (or lack thereof) is dependent on where our attention is directed.

What relates meditation to yoga (union)? When our attention goes beyond thought (meditative state), it can enter the cognitive space of silence where it unites with the deeper self. We will submit later that it also unites our individual attention with the "whole." Importantly, we make the distinction that yoga is a *state* rather than a practice or set of exercises.

## Why meditation?

What can we achieve when we meditate? Can meditation really produce—in the body and brain—a transformational process similar to the one experienced by a computer when it is linked to the internet? Could this be a mechanism that enables us to unveil the depths of our inner qualities—and flourish to our fullest potentials?

Indeed, meditation plays a biological function. Metabolic changes, occurring during the meditative state, produce lower blood pressure and heart and respiratory rates. The concentration of neuromediators, which are responsible for our physical and cognitive (hyper) activity (via chemical substances mainly produced in our brains, such as adrenalin and cortisol)—decreases as well. However, other substances connected to positive emotions, states of calm, and relaxation (e.g., melatonin, serotonin, beta-endorphins, and dopamine) grow in their concentration via the practice of meditation.

Dopamine is an anti-inflammatory painkiller and is part of the "reward system" that we have in our brain. Dopamine levels, in particular, have been shown to be enhanced during meditation, presumably reflecting the "reward" aspect of meditation (e.g., feelings of joy and happiness). In effect, meditation is both a rewarding and rewarded activity. In the state of thoughtless awareness, the brain saves energy and stops the otherwise ceaseless flow of unintentional and mostly superfluous thoughts. One can only marvel at the fact that the brain "celebrates" the achievement of this rare state of alert with a powerful production of joyful emotions via the activation of the dopaminergic system.[32]

Still, even though thoughtless awareness is a natural, spontaneous, and universal experience, you may feel like it has been eluding you. This is because we often do not fully register it. In the Italian language, there is an expression called *sovrappensiero*, meaning "beyond thought." This is a good way to describe the experience of entering the meditative state of consciousness where thoughts slow down and suddenly stop. When we ask our program participants if they have experienced this at all, they confirm they have and, in fact, remember these experiences very well. We often laugh together as we reflect on them and how we find them enjoyable, effortless—and rare. In fact, this type of experience leaves a clear trace in our experiential memory. However, we do not always register this as a specific state of mind. In other words, we may have experienced intense states of happiness (or serenity) but did not know how to retain them and were not aware that we may, in fact, have been in a state of meditation.

The question then naturally arises: is there a way to attain such a state whenever we wish to call upon it and, if so, how do we get to that point?

Evolution is a natural process that occurs over long periods of time; however, at certain critical inflection points, it registers significant progress via "leaps" (a phenomenon some have encapsulated in the oft-used expression "quantum leap"). The question we may ask ourselves is: would such a leap in evolution not happen also within an individual's consciousness?

As a matter of fact it does, as we shall soon see.

We need to emphasize, at this stage, the fact that, while thoughtless awareness can occur spontaneously for short durations, getting to the point where it happens consistently—and over longer periods of time—requires a daily practice of meditation sustained over the course of months and even years.

Another common question in our training programs is: *"Why should one meditate?"* The answer should now be clear from the above discussion on the characteristics of the meditative state of consciousness and what distinguishes meditation from other experiences (e.g., daydreaming and concentration). Meditation offers the opportunity to reach the deepest level of insight within ourselves and as it relates to our surroundings. If we value the aspiration of flourishing (i.e., the realization of our fullest potential), then all we need is a scientific and curious mind. We need to be willing to experiment and verify by ourselves whether and how well our state of consciousness can deepen and broaden.

The more neuroscience evolves and our knowledge deepens via brain imaging studies, the more we realize that our brains can do a myriad of things. However, not all functions are activated at the same time. The practice of meditation promotes the development of qualities that correspond to "aptitude centers," as we will refer in the upcoming chapters to these special locations positioned along our spinal cord and within our brain. The realization of the potential of these centers is critical for the purpose of our evolutionary learning.

There is a long list of reasons why meditation is beneficial to us. However, we'd like to draw attention to one aspect that we believe is particularly important for human beings in general and professionals in particular—specifically, how meditation affects the quality of our limbic system. This area of the brain is central to our decision-making capabilities (in whatever tasks we tackle); it also conditions us in our choices; and, finally, it pushes us in the direction of repeating pleasant experiences and accessing short-term rewards (even if they may not be the best for our health and evolution). Our experience shows that, when individuals establish themselves in meditation, they have entered an optimal state of being. Specifically, they get well, feel it, and thus become eager to repeat the experience; however, they do so without developing an attachment to the experience itself.

This is the main reason why, without any added incentive (e.g., organizational support or income-generating potential), practitioners of "spontaneous meditation" continue to practice it. They enjoy the growing manifestation of this internal reward feedback. More importantly, however, they enjoy the growth in self-awareness that guides them to make the best possible choices (which also turn out to be the most pleasant ones).

This is key for "sustainability-as-flourishing" in organizations. Individual, short-term self-interest can always get in the way of collective long-term performance, which creates a host of sustainability problems. The good news is that we can now develop our capacities to forego immediate rewards and prioritize the long-term common good via shifts in brain reward patterns. This would represent a golden solution towards creating an *effortless, built-in and second-nature mindset of sustainability*. The question is how to develop such a capacity in individuals. Can meditation—a seemingly simple and ancient practice—make this happen?

> **Spontaneous meditation:** a system of meditation based on thoughtless awareness, triggered by the activation and sustenance of an inner "catalytic" energy.

CEL's methodology of choice is a system of "spontaneous meditation" based on thoughtless awareness—a state of consciousness that is enabled via the awakening of an inner energy—*catalytic energy*—which will be discussed in the following chapter. This state generates a condition of general relaxation that reduces the activity of the sympathetic nervous system (which induces tension) and activates the parasympathetic nervous system (which induces relaxation among other things). This state of meditation/thoughtless awareness has been shown[33] to be associated with the activation of the brain's limbic and attention regions. These areas represent neural networks (used for our "internalized" attention) and also constitute triggers for other neural areas that are responsible for positive feelings (hence the reported sense of fulfillment, wellbeing and psycho-emotional balance).

> **Collective consciousness:** the ability to feel or register others on one's central nervous system.

This capacity (i.e., to bring the attention inside and achieve a state of balance and fulfillment) predisposes the individual to broaden the perception of self and include the interests of others, who are increasingly felt as connected beings that are part of the same system. This connectivity (i.e., the ability to feel/register others on one's own central nervous system, in a tangible way similar to our senses perceiving that the sky is blue or the fire is hot) is what we call *collective consciousness* (a term we shall further explore in Chapter 5). Progressively, this broadening collective consciousness generates decisions and actions that create positive behaviors, which are reinforced by positive feedback loops. The system starts moving towards a more sustainable equilibrium; it is propelled by "spontaneous" positive behavior enacted by the meditative brain in its efforts to satisfy the "larger" self.

## Research on meditation

To gain a thorough perspective on the effects of meditation (especially those based on thoughtless awareness), let us review the results of research published in prominent scientific journals across a wide variety of fields.

### Genetic effects

One of the more surprising studies related to meditation stemmed from a collateral but intriguing question: can meditation affect our DNA? A recent study showed that a few hours of meditation during an eight-week study program could influence the expression of our DNA.[34] The authors affirm that "RR (relaxation response) elicitation results in characteristic gene expression changes that can be used to measure physiological responses elicited by the RR in an unbiased fashion." Meditation can control the expression of the genes that regulate inflammation and apoptosis (programmed cell death) as well as the response to free radicals, as stress activates the genes associated with inflammation. This modified genetic expression can lead to long-term physiological effects. The article states that meditation can "turn off" the genes of distress, which is a well-known risk factor for most human diseases (from the common flu to cancer)—and it also states that this effect can be long-lasting.

## Therapeutic effects

A study conducted at McMaster's University in Toronto[35] showed that spontaneous meditation produced significant increases in beta-endorphins, which are related to feelings of happiness and euphoria. In particular, in male subjects, these neurochemicals increased by 70%. Beta-endorphins are also released during high-performance sports, as well as when people are in love. They are thought to play an important role in homeostatic mechanisms, pain reduction, and may even affect the immune system, which could explain why practitioners of this type of meditation experience improvements in severe illnesses such as asthma, high blood pressure, epilepsy, and others.

A study[36] conducted at the Natural Therapies Research Unit of the Royal Hospital for Women in Sydney, Australia (and in collaboration with the Institute of Psychiatry at King's College in London) showed that spontaneous meditation yields significant improvements in the symptoms of Attention Deficit and Hyperactivity Disorder (ADHD). Twenty-six subjects suffering from ADHD practiced meditation over a period of six weeks and were compared to a waiting-list control group who received no treatment. Meditators showed a significant reduction in key symptoms associated with hyperactivity, impulsiveness, and inattention. Other secondary benefits were improved family relationships and enhanced self-esteem. Furthermore, over half of the meditators who had been previously treated with stimulant medication discontinued or reduced their medication while continuing to experience symptom-related improvements.

## Stress reduction

Another study conducted in Sydney, Australia showed the efficacy of the aforementioned type of meditation on reducing stress.[37] The study used quantitative feedback based on the standardized Kessler Psychological Distress Scale (K10) collected before and after a workshop administered to 299 attending physicians who were taught to meditate over a period of two weeks. The results indicated that the method is an "effective mental health promotion and prevention strategy." Among the various metrics collected, the overwhelming majority of participants (over 93%) indicated varying levels of improvement due to the practice of meditation. The areas surveyed were relief from stress, tension and anxiety; mental silence; and calm and peacefulness.

## The neurophysiology of meditation: EEG studies

A study published in the *International Journal of Neuroscience* was the first to demonstrate that long-term practitioners of spontaneous meditation develop a positive sense of detachment as they showed reduced emotional reactivity and increased resilience to stressful events.[38] Specifically, 25 long-term meditators (compared to a control group) showed a reduction in psychological, physiological, and electrophysiological reactivity to stressful stimuli. This was the first study to generate neurophysiological data that supported the hypothesis that meditation leads to emotional balance and greater emotional resilience (associated with stressful life events).

The responses of meditators were compared to controls as they watched a stressful video clip. On a psychological scale, the meditators (vs. controls) showed reduced subjective ratings of negative emotions (e.g., disgust, sadness, anger, and fear) elicited by the movie. They also showed reduced levels of an autonomic indicator of stress (skin-potential levels). At the brain level, the meditators showed reduced gamma activity over their frontal brain regions compared to the control group; gamma wave activity over frontal regions is reflective of increased focused arousal in relation to emotional involvement. These findings provide pioneering neurophysiological evidence for the claim that the long-term effects of spontaneous meditation lead to greater emotional stability, reduced emotional reactivity, and greater resilience to stressful stimuli.

Several EEG studies conducted by Russian scientists between 2001 and 2003[39] compared the brain activation of long- vs. short-term meditation practitioners and found that, during meditation, long-term meditators showed reduced thought activity and more feelings of happiness based on the subjects' own ratings. These studies indicated that the alpha as well as the more rare theta waves—associated with the feeling of happiness or positive emotions—increase as mental activity (thinking) decreases, demonstrating the mental benefits of the state of thoughtless awareness.

Another study published in the *International Journal of Neuroscience* compared 25 practitioners of spontaneous meditation to a similarly sized group of control subjects on a range of trait personality metrics.[40] Long-term meditators scored significantly lower in certain personality features (i.e., anxiety, neuroticism, psychoticism, and depression) and scored higher in emotion recognition and expression, suggesting that the long-term practice of thoughtless awareness leads to greater psycho-emotional stability and better emotional skills. The alarming statistics of antidepressant consumption by youth, in many developed countries, warrant the growth of interest in such research.

## Neurophysiology of meditation: brain imaging studies

Several studies using fMRI[41] have shown that meditation enhances the activation of the brain's regions pertaining to the attention as well as the regions of cognitive control, presumably due to the fact that meditation is a powerful attention training technique and is associated with increased self-control (e.g., inhibiting thoughts). In addition, meditation has been shown to activate limbic areas that mediate and affect motivation control.[42]

The idea of evolution and self-empowerment of the individual as well as of the whole collective is linked to the notion of education. *Co-nascere* ("to be born with") in Latin is the etymological root of cognition—a term used for the knowledge of the self. The Romans referred to the process of knowledge as an extraction, from within, of our skills and talents. As such, education should be the process of discovering ourselves, how we all are similar (as human beings), and how each one of us is a complex individual—and different from everyone else.

The concept of meditation is, in a way, fundamentally the same as the concept of education; however, it goes beyond the exploration of emotions or the generation of thoughts. Thought and emotional processes are found by several studies to be significantly reduced during meditation, leading to a different level of the experience of cognition. This simple observation suggests that we are more than emotion and thought. We can experience more of ourselves, our surroundings, and other human beings; importantly, our level of knowledge and interactions can be broader, wider, and richer than we have known thus far, allowing us to cope better with stressful or quickly changing external conditions.

We believe that this enhanced consciousness of reality could be the main biological purpose of the meditation process and of the state of thoughtless awareness. In fact, we have found that the significant mental, emotional, and physical benefits observed are mere byproducts of this process. At the same time, and in paradoxical contrast to its stillness, meditation is a dynamic state that has a stimulating impact on the brain—a sort of action within inaction.

## Neuroplasticity

A range of studies demonstrate a large number of benefits derived from the practice of meditation; however, some are of specific interest since they indicate improved cognition as a result of neuroplasticity. Neuroplasticity (i.e., a change in brain structure as a result of experience) is considered to be one of the most important discoveries of neuroscience. Over the past decade, evidence has been growing that the brain structure changes in adults in response to the training of specific skills. For example, it is widely known that musicians have larger structures in brain regions that are relevant to the musical instrument they are playing and the music skills they have acquired over the years.

However, more recent research has shown that even a few months of training for a specific skill (e.g., learning a musical instrument, or how to juggle, or studying for an exam) are associated with significant changes in corresponding brain regions. For instance, the hippocampus (which is important for learning and spatial memory) has been shown to be enlarged in taxi drivers in London (who must learn how to navigate the streets) or in students who have spent three intensive months studying for a medical exam. Likewise, juggling for a period of only three months has been shown to enhance the sensorimotor regions of the brain as well as interregional structural connectivity; however, after just a one-month break from juggling, a reversal of structural changes was shown. Thus, the brain is much more plastic than we originally assumed, and this is not only the case for children (whose brain plasticity has been recognized for a long time); use-dependent brain plasticity can also be achieved in adults.

There are strong indications that the practice of meditation has a direct, anatomically visible, and measurable effect on gray and white brain matter as well as on structural brain connectivity. There is extensive literature showing not only growth of both types of matter in specific areas but also enhanced levels of *connection* between different brain regions. Both yoga and meditation practices bring improvements in tasks that require selective and sustained (i) attention, (ii) concentration, (iii) ability to inhibit distraction, (iv) cognitive control, (v) visual scanning abilities, and (vi) repetitive motor responses. A study on the performance of participants in a mirror-tracing exercise found that the yoga/meditation group had improved reversal ability, eye–hand coordination and speed and accuracy, which were necessary for mirror star tracing.

Several studies have analyzed the neuroplasticity of brain structures in relation to the long-term practice of meditation. They used different structural imaging approaches (e.g., measuring brain activation, gray matter, or white matter volume increase in meditators vs. non-meditators) and showed that brain connections, which reflect neuronal communication, are changed in a positive way in long-term meditators compared to novices.

When researchers looked at yoga and meditation practitioners (YMPs) and a sample of well-matched controls, they saw significant differences in both gray matter volume and self-reported cognitive failures.[43] YMPs exhibited volumetrically larger brain structures and fewer lapses in the executive function in daily life. Structural differences were particularly evident in brain regions with higher-order control of cognitive and motor responses. At the same time, the extent to which the meditators and control group differed with regard to gray matter volume in these regions was significantly associated with the occurrence of self-reported cognitive failures.[44]

One study compared long-term meditators with matched control participants and found that meditators (vs. non-meditators) had larger gray matter volume in brain areas that are associated with emotional regulation and response control (i.e., the right orbitofrontal cortex [OFC] and right hippocampus). Furthermore, long-term meditators had overall greater amounts of gray matter (which normally decreases with age). This suggests that meditators may develop "younger," i.e., more precise, plastic, integrative, brains.[45] This study showed increased gray matter in the left hippocampus of the meditators group, a brain area strongly involved in learning and memory. After only four weeks of meditation, changes in white matter (which is involved in interconnecting brain areas) were present in participants who meditated, but not in control participants who engaged in relaxation exercises. Interestingly, these changes involved also the anterior cingulate cortex, a part of the brain that contributes to self-regulation. This is a particularly important aspect when it comes to sustainability-as-flourishing, since the key to sustainable decision-making and action is to be able to resist the temptation to access immediate rewards (i.e., short-term profit, a large bonus at the end of the year) in exchange for higher and more stable long-term rewards.

## Individual flourishing through meditation

In our Proposition 1 we suggest that there is a direct link between the learning and practice of spontaneous meditation and the development of a managerial mindset that is oriented towards sustainable decision-making and actions. However, is sustainability-as-flourishing learnable through a meditation-based learning intervention? To respond to this question, a randomized controlled trial of spontaneous meditation vs. (computer-based) cognitive training was designed where study participants were compared to a passive control group. The objective of the study was to determine the effectiveness of these two forms of learning as it relates to the development of sustainability-related behavior. This was a joint research program[46] between Bocconi University's research center dedicated to management studies and the cognitive neuroscience research center of San Raffaele University in Milan, Italy. CEL was charged with the design and delivery of the meditation training.

The learning intervention yielded a wide range of outcomes. Firstly, it indicated a significant reduction in fatigue and nervousness and an enhancement in the levels of satisfaction, self-confidence, and general wellbeing. Secondly, certain key personal value dimensions for sustainability-as-flourishing (e.g., self-transcendence and cooperativeness) increased significantly during the meditation learning program. Thirdly (and most directly related to flourishing behavior), the decisions made during a business simulation—in the form of a classic "tragedy-of-commons" problem[47]—showed a significant difference in managerial decisions and long-term performance outcomes for participants undergoing the meditation learning intervention. They resisted the temptation to maximize short-term profits and were thus able to maximize long-term rewards for both their company and their industry sector. This phenomenon did not occur, in terms of pre/post learning differences, in the control samples.

Finally, brain imaging (fMRI) techniques showed that meditative training produced an increase in the gray matter density, similar to the study reported above, in the anterior cingulate cortex which is linked to attentional control and conflict resolution, as well as on the right inferior frontal gyrus connected to emotional self-regulation and behavioral flexibility. The net effect was predisposing participants to resist the temptation of accessing immediate rewards and adapting their behaviors in favor of commonly shared—as well as individually enjoyed—benefits.

## Final considerations

The notion of plasticity of the brain sustains the core assumption presented in this book that our capacity for knowledge is part of an evolutionary process. In the years to come, further research in the fields of psychology and neurosciences may confirm the findings of epigenetics, casting more light on the manner in which behavior in general and meditation in particular changes the expression and/or activation of specific genes.

This brief incursion into the domain of the brain's endocrinology supports the fact that, at this stage of human evolution, we realize that we can know more, know better, and that we can affect, in a non-trivial manner, the way in which we are knowing. Brain plasticity implies that the mere act of acquiring knowledge is evolutionary; as we become more aware of the world around us, we can simultaneously enhance the quality of our environment and our inner capacity to sense it. Thus, the new territory to discover (after crossing the ocean of information, concepts, ideas, and assumptions) is consciousness itself.

We explore this via an *expanded category of perception*. If such a cognitive function exists and is triggered, could this phenomenon be simple, natural, and spontaneous, akin to all other vital functions such as breathing and digestion? This would go significantly beyond traditional meditation and concentration exercises. As we shall see in the following chapters, there is emerging evidence that the answer to this question is affirmative.

# 4
# The inner transformation engine

"To move beyond the confusion of complexity, executives must abandon their constant search for the immediately practical and, paradoxically, seek to understand the underlying ideas and values that have shaped the world they work in. Managers who clamor for how-to instructions are, by definition, stuck on the near side of complexity."

**Oliver Wendell Holmes**

In the previous chapter, we reviewed neuroscientific evidence on the effectiveness of meditative practices. We contend that these practices support the manifestation of an evolutionary leap towards flourishing. In particular, we have learned that meditation produces significant neuroplasticity effects in the brains of practitioners; this, in turn, translates into expressions of values, emotions, and decisions that increasingly align with the concept of individual flourishing (defined in Chapter 1).

But how and why does this happen? What is the underlying mechanism that induces meditation practitioners to experience deep structural changes in the brain and spontaneously modify the way they make decisions in the context of sustainability dilemmas? Why is meditation such a powerful tool for achieving significant change in the way people make relevant business decisions? In this chapter and the next one, we set out to explore this inner mechanism—the engine inside human beings that powers this transformation we have called the evolutionary leap to a flourishing state. However, we will now tackle the matter from an entirely different standpoint: that of wisdom traditions. Meditation practices, in fact, have been developed in many cultural traditions across time. They have brought to light new perspectives—some have been validated, some have not yet been explained scientifically, and many can be tested via suitable practices (individually and at a mass scale), as we will see shortly.

Admittedly, readers will find some convergence between this enquiry and other fields of exploration (e.g., psychology or spirituality), and they are correct. Today, science and spirituality are on a converging course.[48] Of course, we are not referring to the doctrinarian spirituality of traditional religions but to experimental spirituality that investigates processes of energies and consciousness—a field where contemporary scientists are also venturing. Given the intricacies of the subject matter, we felt that adopting such an interdisciplinary approach would be best suited to help us gain a better perspective.

## Ancient traditions and modern views

There is a long and significant history of experimentation and knowledge that deals with (i) the subtle and spiritual aspects of the energetic body (and its correspondences with various organs and the nervous system) and (ii) elevated states of consciousness attained in meditative states. A detailed exploration of such matters could comprise another book and is thus not within the scope of the present work; however, we would still like to provide a few examples from the ancient to the modern.

Patanjali's classical yoga treatise alludes, in Book I, to *yoga* (union) being identical to thoughtless awareness: "Yoga is the suppressing of the thought-streams" (literally: waves of the mind, *Yogas chitta-vritti-nirodhah*).[49] Also, ancient texts of yoga described self-realization as the awakening of the catalytic energy (*Kundalini* in Sanskrit) through the aptitude centers (chakras) and thus leading to thoughtless awareness: "When the Kundalini is sleeping it will be aroused ... Then all the chakras and knots are pierced and prana [life force] flows through the royal road of Sushumna [central flow of energy—parasympathetic nervous system]. The mind is released from its work."[50] *The Zohar* refers to the stars and planets of the body hidden under the skin,[51] the seven pillars,[52] and the central channel of ascension, which is the mystery of mysteries where all "ladders" arrive and unite into one.[53] Plato describes the left, right, and central channels of energy in the body as running alongside the backbone and indicates that they are interlocked at the level of the head.[54]

Closer to present times, Victor Mair showed that

> there are so many correspondences between Yoga and Taoism—even in the smallest and oddest detail—throughout the history of their development that we might almost think of them as two variants of a single ... philosophical system. Both conceive of conduits, tracts, channels, or arteries through which the vital breath, or energy, flows. They view the main channel as originating in the "root", or "tail", region of the body, then passing through the spinal column and flanked by two subsidiary channels ... Both Yoga and Taoism maintain that there are certain points in the body where energy is held, or bound, and that there are supports that guide the vital breath. Both acknowledge the existence of "wheels or fields" of this energy.[55]

By measuring certain physical parameters, an American researcher reached conclusions that confirmed the existence of the chakras. Dr. Zaboj V. Harvalik (a physicist who was a scientific adviser to the U.S. Army's Advanced Material Concepts Agency) claimed that "these measurements suggest that dowsing sensors must be located in the region of the solar plexus and that perhaps there are additional sensors in the head or brain."[56] William Tiller, chairman of the Department of Material Science at Stanford University, referred to the chakras when he wrote: "These seven endocrine centers have been called our sacred centers and through them we radiate transmitting information of a quality (frequency) associated with that center."[57]

In 1970, Shri Mataji Nirmala Devi, a globally recognized spiritual leader and teacher of meditation who was born in India in 1923, began sharing the knowledge and related practice of an inner transformation method she called as Sahaja yoga. This type of yoga is based on the activation of an inner energy (*Kundalini,* catalytic energy) which enables a meditative state where thoughtless awareness is reached and gradually developed. This formed the foundation of the spontaneous meditation methodology adopted by CEL, which incorporates some of the ancient knowledge about energy (aptitude) centers and energy flows (channels) that Shri Mataji brought to new levels of profundity, detail, and relevance for contemporary societies. (We will return to this topic later in this chapter.)

## The inner energetic system

As introduced in Chapter 1, our hypothesis is that certain types of deep meditative practices enable a shift in individual consciousness towards systemic views that embed "sustainability-as-flourishing" into everyday decisions and actions. The shift is possible because meditation is a tool to access, explore, and manifest inner qualities, personality traits, and energy flows that allow the flourishing of individuals. This inestimable inner wealth is normally latent or not immediately accessible; to access and manifest it, we need to start our "inner transformation engine" and learn how to operate it.

The following pages will clarify the structure of this inner mechanism and its way of functioning. Secondly, we will learn how individual inner energy flows can be accessed and mastered to activate flourishing qualities, aptitudes, and behaviors. The following chapter will explore how to expand from individual empowerment to collective flourishing.

The figure below uses Leonardo da Vinci's Vitruvian man to illustrate the structure of the energetic transformation engine, which (according to several wisdom traditions) resides within every human being. The diagram highlights the system of the three *energy flows* or channels (disposed vertically) and seven *aptitude centers* that power the inner transformation process. The gray vertical line, on the left side of the body, represents the left sympathetic nervous system (SNS); the white line, at the right of the spine (from the perspective of the person depicted), represents the right SNS; and the central line passing through the spine represents the parasympathetic nervous system (PNS). The potential, dormant, fourth energy—the *catalytic energy*—is depicted as a spiral with 3½ coils in the triangular bone called *sacrum* (at the base of the spine).

**FIGURE 10.** A representation of the inner transformation engine

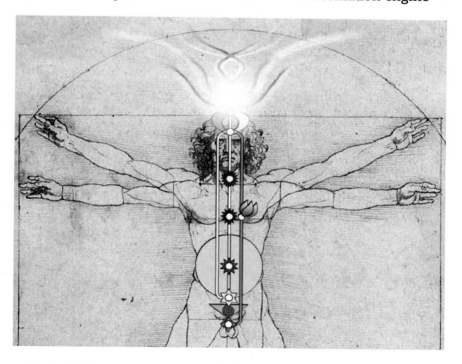

In the following sections, we will explain (i) the characteristics of the energy flows, (ii) the characteristics of the aptitude centers, and (iii) the conditions necessary to "start the engine."

## The triple energy flow

According to wisdom traditions from both Eastern (Hindu, Buddhism, Taoism, and Confucianism) and Western (Christian mysticism, Sufism, Jewish Kabala, and Hopi Indians) civilizations, a system of energies exists within us; some can be connected with the functioning of our central nervous system. In essence, we are equipped with a vertical superimposition of seven essential aptitude centers (*chakras* in Sanskrit), which are wired together by an intricate neural network. They receive, distribute, and manage three types of energies, which translate into aptitudes and talents specific to each aptitude center. Thus, they also sustain core behavioral and flourishing capacities.

The three main flows of energy that enable human beings to operate and run their lives have been a recurrent theme in Indian cosmology (e.g., the *Bhagavad Gita*) and Chinese Taoism (e.g., the notions of Yin–Yang and Tao). In the 19th century they were rediscovered by Hegelian and Marxist thought (action, reaction, and synthesis). This triple structure was projected in Hegel's *Phenomenology of the Spirit* and inspired modern political philosophy (as demonstrated for example in Mao Tse Tung's *Essay on Contradiction*).[58]

The Hegelian triad describes the essential nature of these three energy flows, which were yet again rediscovered by neuroscience in association with the SNS (sympathetic nervous system) and PNS (parasympathetic nervous system). The SNS is responsible for the "fight or flight" response within animals and humans. Since the SNS is a reactive system, it is called into play in cases of emergency and upset, for the purpose of protection. Its two main functions are to suppress (left SNS) and activate (right SNS). The PNS counteracts both the suppression and activation energies of SNS via the so-called relaxation effect.[59] From a psychological point of view, the suppressive energy of the left channel (Yin) generates superego and the activation energy of the right channel (Yang) generates ego. Moods and emotions originate from the energy flow on the left side and thoughts and volition are released from the energy flow on the right side.

Sympathetic reflexes can trigger powerful physiological reactions to help us confront changes, threats, and challenges in our environment (e.g., heart and respiratory rates increase, adrenal glands activate, and muscles contract). The PNS creates a restorative force that brings the body back into equilibrium after the startling effects of the sympathetic reflexes. It is interconnected with all of the body's vital senses and organs, and reposes the body by equalizing the activity levels of all organs. During a PNS response, heart and lung rates slow down, adrenal glands rest, and muscles relax.

We now proceed to take a closer look at the three energy flows, which are responsible for many of the dynamics that take place inside the individual as well as the organization.

## First energy flow: left-side sympathetic nervous system (left SNS)

"I am I plus my circumstances."

**José Ortega y Gasset**

According to Eastern traditions, the two first energy flows act as "thermo-regulators" of our personalities. The first one (moon channel [i.e., Yin in China and Ida Nadi in India]) corresponds to the left-side SNS; its main role is to cool down our temperaments (e.g., it reduces tendencies towards anger, impulsive reactions, and hasty decisions), which yields more introverted and static personality traits and attitudes. This area of our consciousness stores the weight of the past and our connection to our emotional beings, and contains acquired knowledge and traditions, conditionings, and habits. On the positive side, we can benefit from positive enriching habits, the support of closely knit communities, and the inherited corporate culture—or, on the negative side, we can be bound by prejudices, superstitions, and attachments to outdated doctrines and theories.

Ancient traditions consider the heart to be the ruling organ of the left energy flow, which is connected to our motivation and desire. This is one of the pillars of leadership, since desires signify our purpose and activate the energy needed for taking action; they also enable us to move with full conviction and occasional passion. A committed purposefulness (to reaching goals) will endow leaders with the capacity to attain their strategic visions.

In terms of individual flourishing, the left SNS activates the power of the heart. Since our wellbeing depends on the capacity to enjoy, this is linked to the heart. The left SNS energy flow nourishes a natural tendency to be content, maintain friendly relationships (and an agreeable working atmosphere), handle the power of emotions, and thus become an asset within communities, families, and work environments. Some of the advantages that come with the optimal functioning of the first energy flow include an easy propensity to enjoy, the deft articulation of an individual in relation to a collective background, and an identity that is at peace with oneself. Emotional maturity is derived from self-confidence and the capacity to connect.

Opposite dimension when this energy flow is not in balance
The left SNS terminates in the right side of the brain, at the level of the optic chiasm. This section of the right hemisphere is a storehouse of memories, habits, and conditionings and generates the "superego." In this context, we might consider the superego as a byproduct of the surplus of activities associated with the energy flows on the left side. When the left SNS flow is blocked, we feel as if we are "going into reverse" (i.e., lacking a sense of purpose or direction). Movement often carries the weight of inertia and passivity. The superego and left energy flow, if out of balance, can also create fear. In this context, the organizational culture becomes subservient and tends towards stagnation and decay. Positive trends are erased by the blandness of routine, deceitfulness, and slyness, expressed through backstabbing and sabotage. One starts seeing problems instead of solutions; depression and despair may surface in more extreme cases. When this energy flow stagnates, tendencies are more self-destructive and result in lackluster performances of individuals and corporations.

## Second energy flow: right-side sympathetic nervous system (right SNS)

"Consider how dark life would be if man in his confusion would become his own sun."

**Goethe**

The second energy flow of the right SNS (sun channel [i.e., Yang in China and Pingala Nadi in India]) beneficially warms up the system to keep pace with a dynamic motion (away from the burden of weariness, tiredness, or dejection). This attitude is extroverted and outgoing. This energy flow enables us to project, act, and express ourselves. Art, science, and startup companies emerge as byproducts of the activation of this energy flow. Lightness and humor brighten the path. We are within the world of thought, action, creativity, enthusiasm, and dynamism; we expand our outreach and aim at excellence.

Ancient traditions describe the liver as the ruling organ of the energy flow on the right side, which is thought to sustain our creative energy. This is key, since our sense of satisfaction depends on the expression of our creativity and achieving our objectives; if this energy flow is positively channeled, we are driven, daring, result-oriented, and belong to a category of people who leave a footprint on this earth. The sky is the limit. We do; we dare.

Thus, it is no surprise that individuals and organizations have considered this second energy flow to be the preferred mode of operation because of the results it produces. However, how does a leader remain the master of action? True, when commitment is felt (based on the first energy flow), it can express itself via qualities of discipline and willpower (cultivated through this second energy flow). However, control of others does not mean self-control. Furthermore, while organizations need a hierarchy, individuals primed for power are also more likely to break the rules. While those who recognize the dark side of power tend to avoid it, withdrawing is not enough to be a master of action.

To remain fully aware of the wider picture, our focus should not be limited to the fruits of our own actions. Qualities that are critical for striking the right balance and attaining success include (i) detachment from results, (ii) critical scrutiny of one's desires and actions, and (iii) stepping back and seeing the big picture. The properties of the third energy flow become essential for attaining this.

Opposite dimension when this energy flow is not in balance

The right SNS terminates in the left side of the brain after crossing over at the level of the optic chiasm. This section of the left hemisphere corresponds to the ego. In this context, we might consider the ego as a byproduct of a surplus of activities on the right side.

Ego-driven action tends to be linear (going off on a tangent and away from the central axis of sustenance), lacks flexibility, and can easily be disconnected from its associated environments (because the fine perceptiveness of wider empathy is missing). Furthermore, the ego pushes forward, no matter what, due to its need for self-gratification. However, in today's fast- and ever-changing world, we sorely need the ability to adapt. Adaptation is one of the characteristics of evolution, which is a spiral movement that continuously adjusts direction while arriving at higher and higher states.

Allegories of linearity can be found in history, notably in the life of military commanders (e.g., Napoleon marching his faithful troops on Moscow, a city too far and cold). Power can be addictive; however, when people push things too far, they are blinded by their own sun channels (e.g., Nazism or fascism are instances of sunstrokes on the sun channel). Individuals who rely too heavily on this ego-boosting energy miss the point and hurt others. Excesses in the use of this energy of the right-side SNS lead to multiple forms of aggression and the science of exploitation. This tendency is destructive to society in a myriad of ways: hubris, domination, obliviousness to the motivations of others, and overlooking the needs of the environment. Destruction of the natural environment (and of the communities surrounding an enterprise) can also result from unbridled ego. Stories abound of heartless work environments that produce daily hassles, stress, maladies, and employees who are pushed to extremes (for instance, in the ranks of middle managers at France Telecom there were on average two suicides per month for over 1½ years around the start of the Great Recession).

The dual forces of the SNS, captured by these two complementary flows of inner energies, are as old as humankind. They influence us daily (whether we are aware of it or not), carry our desire and will, and they also distort our perception of reality as they carry their own momentum. A back-and-forth oscillation between the two poles represented by the left and right SNS energies leads us to repeat the same mistakes, fosters cyclical patterns of wrong decisions, and prevents paradigm shifts and the achievement of sustainable, adaptive changes. These two energy channels eventually breed compelling but misleading emotions (such as delusional lines of thinking). This can lead to the phenomenon of enantiodromia, which means that an extreme trend can yield the contrary outcome; we strive without achieving. The Buddhists describe a consequence of this see-saw movement (between left and right) as the ocean of illusion—an ocean without shores, alternatively described as an ocean where reaching one shore invariably sends you swimming back towards the other one.

Progress, in so many areas of human endeavor, is based on an everlasting quest for the attainment of balance on the third channel of energy—a pursuit of harmony and synthesis, which remains elusive. In fact, the third (PNS) energy flow can be opened only via an ascending dialectic (spiral) movement, based on the activation of the fourth (catalytic) energy which will be described shortly.

## Third energy flow: parasympathetic nervous system (PNS)

> "Wise people, even if all laws were abolished, would still lead the same life."
>
> **Aristophanes**

Our spine is critical for our neurological and holistic health as it hosts the PNS and associated third energy flow, which plays a major role in our capacity to expand our consciousness.

But how do we adapt to a constantly changing reality? How does an individual, aspiring to a flourishing state, pursue the search for equilibrium in environments that are often chaotic? This is obviously not a trivial question. Sustainability and the preservation of essential ecosystem services are predicated on reconciling the opposites and bridging the gaps of many contradictions.

Set in a specific temporal and spatial location, we must assume the dynamics of change but integrate them with sustainability (seen here as the dynamics of an ever-changing but possible harmony). We are divided by our temperaments between those who gaze back and those who look ahead; as it turns out, we simply need to seize the present—and here comes the delicate balancing act.

The central energy channel (Sushumna Nadi in Sanskrit) brings us closer to attaining "balance" as it opens the point of synthesis and the ability to reach equilibrium on the middle path (as referenced in Buddhist teachings). The space associated with this energy channel carries the synthesis of harmony between the dual forces of the right and left sides. This energy flow enables us to navigate and strike a balance between desire and thought, between commitment and detachment. Our self-regulating framework helps us advance with confident footing (avoiding to cross behavioral boundaries that could become self-destabilizing or extreme). Furthermore, we can spot—walking along this middle path—the outline of the Confucian superior person (ginza) equipped with the five perfect virtues.[60]

The search for the third energy flow represents a quest for harmony and truth. We see these qualities synthesized, for instance, in the aesthetics and philosophy of ancient Greece. The harmonious flow of this force works for "sustainability as preservation" and "sustainability as renewal." Furthermore, the third energy flow powers a self-propelled autonomy, enables us to see ahead of the curve, and focuses on learning and evolving (opening the conduit that sustains transformation and ascent).

Access to this all-important central energy flow is not generally within the reach of our volition because it is dependent on the PNS. However, one of the chief purposes of meditation is to open this third channel. Thus, while the left SNS engenders emotions from the past (right-brain hemisphere) and the right SNS generates future-oriented thoughts (left-brain hemisphere), the central energy flow corresponds

# 4 THE INNER TRANSFORMATION ENGINE

to the present moment where reality is apprehended directly (without the interceding of emotion or thought).

Let us emphasize this essential point: there are various types of meditation. As described in Chapter 3, spontaneous meditation (in thoughtless awareness) is a meta-mental condition of the consciousness. In other words, it takes us beyond the mind of thoughts and emotions. However, a state beyond the mind cannot be achieved by the activity of the mind and thus mindfulness does not deliver, by definition, the full potential of meditation. In fact, methods based on concentration or visualization techniques are reported to have limited effects.[61]

In the condition of thoughtless awareness, the "here and now" awareness exists continually in the absence of the thought process. Thoughtless awareness is normally a very difficult state to achieve—it is hidden behind a tight locking system that we mostly experience as a barrage of thoughts; to pierce through this, we need extra help. Fortunately, this option is already built into our inner energy system. In fact, the ability to access thoughtless awareness can be greatly facilitated by the (catalytic) energy associated with evolutionary transformation, which creates the conditions for renewal and brings forth the pace of progress and growth, as we will see in the next section.

## Opposite dimension when this energy flow is weak or not in balance

The blockage of the elusive central channel leaves us at the mercy of the oscillations between the left and right PNS. The influence of the two channels onto our mind produces what Buddhism has called the virtual world of illusions (a key theme in the movie *The Matrix*). The third channel, the "Third Way," has fascinated political thinkers from Karl Marx to Tony Blair; however, under normal conditions, it remains elusive. We are stuck with the incapacity to absorb subtler knowledge and to reconcile diverging viewpoints, a difficulty to adapt, a tendency to lose balance in favor of extreme solutions, and to become enmeshed in contradictions that lead to uncertainty and the "fog of war." The pathology of confused minds is a familiar feature in history's tribulations and long chains of missed opportunities.

### Starting the engine: the catalytic energy (fourth energy)

Attempts to unlock the power of the right-side SNS (physical and mental activity) through the power of the left side (heart, emotions) have generated various empathy-training programs and other methodologies that emphasize the cultivation of compassion and kindness. However, whether we join sitting classes, retreat seminars or communication programs, we find it hard to escape the constraints of the interactions at the level of the two energy flows that feed the two hemispheres of the brain.

What does it take to activate the balancing, nurturing, and flourishing power of the central channel (i.e., to start/ignite the inner transformation engine)? Beyond the three energy flows of the left and right SNS and the PNS, there is a remaining and untouched potential energy that packs evolutionary force. Nearly all of the important wisdom traditions developed by humanity across time have described the existence of a subtle energy which is normally dormant at the base of our spine and can be activated under specific conditions. This energy has been given different names: (a) *Kundalini* in India, (b) *Ruh* in the Islam and Sufi traditions, (c) *Chi* in Taoism, (d) *Ki* in Japanese Buddhism, (e) *Shekina* in the Jewish lore, and (f) the cool wind of the Holy Ghost in the esoteric Christian tradition.

In his lectures on the psychology of Kundalini yoga, Carl Jung explained: "You see, the Kundalini in psychological terms is that which makes you go on the greatest adventures . . . It is the quest that makes life livable, and this is Kundalini."[62] "Kundalini, which is to be awakened in the sleeping Mooladhara world, is the suprapersonal, the non-ego . . . For this reason, Kundalini is the same principle as the *Soter*, the Savior Serpent of the Gnostics."[63]

The activation (or awakening) of this energy has been called by many names (e.g., self-realization in English, *Moksha* in Sanskrit and *Satori* in Japanese) and has traditionally taken place under the direct supervision of a master. Such a qualified master first of all had to have this energy awakened within himself or herself, and secondly had to be able to guide its awakening in others. This normally entails a long and assiduous process of purification via a variety of practices (e.g., described in Patanjali's treatises) over periods of time measured in years and even decades, with no guarantees of success. Needless to say, such a feat is virtually impossible for the vast majority of us living modern-day, fast-paced lifestyles.

However, as mentioned earlier in this chapter, Shri Mataji Nirmala Devi created a method of meditation based on thoughtless awareness which is achieved via the awakening of the catalytic energy. She has explained that human consciousness has reached, in our modern times, a level where this awakening can take place spontaneously in any individual—without the long preparation often associated with its attainment. Through the traditional method, one had to purify oneself completely before the energy rose in its fullness (think of the Buddha achieving complete enlightenment under the banyan tree after many years of asceticism); however, via this new method, only a few "threads" of the catalytic energy would rise (because our energetic body has not undergone through the requisite assiduous purification to allow for a full awakening to take place at this initial stage). Fortunately, this is sufficient for the journey of inner transformation towards flourishing to begin.

We found through our own experiences—and through the experiences shared by thousands of our program participants—that this method of spontaneous awakening of the catalytic energy is a very gentle, subtle happening, with remarkable implications for the evolution of our consciousness; however, such implications become apparent only after a certain period of regular meditative practice. This development can be compared to the process of sprouting a seed. The seed only needs to be placed in the soil; however, once it sprouts through its innate properties (and the capability of the earth to make it sprout), it needs care (water) to help it grow into a tree. The water can be likened to the time we allocate, daily, to meditate and nurture the growth of the flow of catalytic energy within us and the purification of the seven aptitude centers, which we will describe shortly. This process leads, over time, to a transformation in our cognitive capabilities that we have described as *collective consciousness* (a subject we will explore in the next chapter).

The availability of this method of spontaneous awakening of the catalytic energy has opened new horizons in diverse domains such as medicine, neuroscience, and academic studies (in the areas of sustainability and organizational development). Some of the possibilities, based on this discovery, are presented within the case studies in Chapter 2 and the neuroscientific research in Chapter 3. Of course, other traditional methods for activating the catalytic energy (i.e., those done in the past) remain viable alternatives; however, they necessitate much longer and strenuous efforts, as described earlier.

We call this power "catalytic" since it actualizes a potential for the evolution of consciousness. When activated, the catalytic energy can trigger (and subsequently sustain) a positive transformation on multiple levels of our being. This energy then begins to flow back to the various aptitude centers, purifying them and awakening their sterling qualities in us in a spontaneous, natural way.

> Catalytic energy: located in the sacrum bone and normally in a dormant state, it can activate an inner transformation via the PNS, which includes the enabling of collective consciousness in the individual.

Firstly, it enhances our sensory perceptions, whereby one's own energetic state as well as the state of another individual can be ascertained. This new category of perception is expressed in thoughtless awareness through the sensitivity to "vibrations"—an approximate translation of the Sanskrit word *Chaitanya* (which is the manifestation of the catalytic energy as a gentle cool breeze that can be felt on the palms and above the top of the head).

Secondly, the catalytic energy can be directed to correct imbalances and weaknesses within the energetic system via simple meditation techniques which engender a healing of our physical, mental, and emotional selves. Thirdly, when this restorative function deploys its effects, the same energy begins to infuse the aptitude centers as we shall see shortly; it also activates their respective qualities or "virtues," which begin to manifest effortlessly. The spontaneous development of these virtues (via the activation of the catalytic energy and regular practice of meditation in thoughtless awareness) constitutes the concrete meaning of individual flourishing. To understand this important aspect, we will now proceed to briefly review the innate qualities associated with each of the aptitude centers.

## Individual flourishing

> "What the superior man seeks is in himself; what the small man seeks is in others."
>
> **Confucius**

> "What lies behind us and what lies before us are tiny matters compared to what lies within us."
>
> **Ralph Waldo Emerson**

Man's inner cognitive instrument is a continent to be further explored by modern science. Values and energies are stored within us, in addition to these flows of energy. Seven centers exist in all human beings, some of them located within the spine, some in the head. They carry these values, representing different qualities and they contain at a seminal level the true potential of our being.

These psychosomatic plexuses are called *chakras* in Sanskrit as they are perceived as rotating wheels of energy. In this context, we will call them *aptitude centers* to emphasize the notion that we can cultivate and develop these properties. Indeed, we submit that, through self-development, we can help awaken the energies or restore the values, conditions, and performance of the aptitude centers.

> Aptitude center: one of seven energy centers located along the spine and in the brain, embodying various human aptitudes and corresponding, on the physical level, to nervous plexuses.

The following presentation of these centers illustrates how dormant aptitudes can flourish into new-found talents and skills for a member of an organization and directly affect the conduct of daily business.

### First aptitude center. Physical expression: pelvic plexus

The most important element of an organism is not always the most visible (e.g., consider the importance of roots to a tree). Individuals and corporations benefit when they are grounded and stable on a consistent basis. Such grounding, in our fundamental nature, manifests in spontaneity, freshness, originality, and magnetism, which provide a sense of gravity and orientation. Gravity has the connotation of natural authority; however, magnetism contains the dual capacity to attract and be attracted. The first aptitude center (*Mooladhara* in Sanskrit) is directly connected with the energy flow of desire (left SNS), which determines the direction of our volition, choices, and actions. Having a good memory is also an endowment of this center.

The first center must be understood as the fundamental platform of the personality; it stores the seeds associated with our capacities, talents, and aptitudes. This platform sustains the primary identity of an individual (or corporation) and can enable evolutions via attunement with one's own gravity center. The first center also sustains the awakening of four core properties.

First, the *quality of authenticity* comes from (i) touching our own depth, (ii) liberating our personality from external influences, (iii) facilitating an identification with what is right (and going to work well for us), and (iv) establishes, on an emotional level, the essence of security. The genuine self that we manifest, in association with our own roots, shields us from various forms of aggression and manipulation. A magnetic personality carries a natural effectiveness, is an expression of positive leadership, and can bring out the best (i.e., flourishing) capacities in others.

The second quality is *wisdom*. This is a notion that is not easy to describe. Is this intelligence without ego? Perhaps. Wisdom is a deep and subtle intelligence, which awakens in us before we can even begin to think, helps us maintain a sense of reality in practical and strategic matters, and is an innate knowledge that synthesizes our sensitivity to sincerity and the common good. We can make the right decisions with incomplete information via this intuitive aptitude. Wisdom enables the expression of common sense; in this state of mind, an individual is in constant touch with his or her inner self and associated realities. Wisdom is often associated with moderation and balance (the qualities of the central channel) and is, in fact, connected to the left SNS; thus, it greatly influences the soundness of our desires.

Thirdly, *discipline* is an aspect of grounded and stable personalities. It is a self-cultivated quality that brings resilience and strength and can help us navigate the waves of our emotions. We are prepared to face external challenges and hardships via the application of discipline, and to stoically maintain consistency—even in a sea of changing circumstances.

Fourthly, although *humility* does not seem to be a popular attribute these days, it is a wonderful character trait that protects us from self-deception and is the corollary of true strength (which does not need the artificial boost of ego pampering). We do not waste our energy on narcissistic self-promotion that will typically generate the criticism and jealousy of others. Humility entails a silent confidence, is based on an awareness that being oneself is enough and can combat hostile dynamics. When one does not overplay one's hand (e.g., by overselling oneself), the personality gains in recognition from those with whom it interacts. The acceptance and credibility of such a personality invite the loyalty of others.

A combination of these four properties sets the stage for the integrated manifestation of aptitudes that emerge at the level of the other psychosomatic centers. An individual can assume his or her own place in an often complex system and understand it. Such individuals are (i) strong and confident in expressing their own nature with sobriety, (ii) experience the all-implicit fullness of a wise perception (of both the known and unknown), and (iii) behave as dynamic personalities—carrying themselves with ease and enjoying their own existence on a path towards the flourishing state.

Opposite dimension when this aptitude is out of balance or weak

Myriad negative outcomes can occur when this aptitude is lacking. Inconsistencies in personalities can undermine authority and credibility. Desires can become destructive (since we do not always wish for what is good for us). Unstable natures may express indecisiveness or overcompensate via aggressive behaviors. Confused behavior, a lack of focus, self-indulgence, and frivolity can cause mistakes and uncertainties.

At a more collective level, the harm done by hampering the expression of this center is deeply rooted and erodes the foundation of humanism. Myriad societal occurrences illustrate the loss of these fundamental values (e.g., the manipulation of children via consumerism, slicing of genomes and organisms in ownership patents, "terminator" technologies, and the ultimate denial of life as a value in itself).

### Second aptitude center. Physical expression: aortic plexus

> "Imagination is more important than knowledge."
>
> **Albert Einstein**

Creative intelligence shapes the world. The second aptitude center (*Swadhishthana* in Sanskrit) is a psychosomatic sensor and receives the energy of creation and nature. The doer, thinker, builder, artist, and entrepreneur depend on this aptitude center because it is directly connected to an energy flow (right-side SNS) that is primarily associated with thought and action. At this center, desire transforms into willpower, the direction is forward and the mode is vigorous. Thus, this center is the "dynamo" of the body; our attention supports it like a radar system. The second center awakens the urge for action and ambition to shape the future within individuals. It enables companies to expand and earnings to rise, and counteracts corporate sloth and stagnation. Finally, it feeds our growth, such as our propensities to develop, build or lead, and stores stamina, fortitude, and creativity.

A basic endowment of this center is a sharp awareness, which manifests as the ability to concentrate and learn easily. Furthermore, sharpness of attention and concentration mobilizes a quick analytical mastery. Specifically, we develop decisiveness in action, conceptual alertness, and a sense for structure and systems. We adhere to reason and become highly capable of inventiveness and inspiration. The second center allows us to move with ease "in" and "out" of the box, as it nourishes both spaces (i.e., rational thinking and imagination). Moreover, and importantly, we are endowed with aesthetics; thus, an innate sense of design and beauty graces our work and products.

Creative intelligence is, in essence, productive. The business world operates through the energy of this center. A corporation cannot be flourishing if it is not functional, industrious, diligent, and occasionally daring. The steady flow of this force of action nourishes eagerness, strong productivity levels, and a high level of performance over the long term. We assert our will and have the capacity to counter malpractices and willful manipulations.

The ability to see ahead of the curve increases with the awakening of this aptitude, which supports competitiveness and technological breakthroughs. Typically, this type of nimble mind will focus on mobility, revamping structures and opening new markets. These valued aptitudes propel growth, expansion, innovation, new business models, products, and services. Companies utilize such innovations to command price premiums, conquer new market segments, reinvent value propositions, accelerate experimentation with strategic options, and utilize business incubators to hatch new models. Interestingly, the West is now breeding startups at an unprecedented rate and emerging-market corporations are going global with untold financial might.

Opposite dimension when this aptitude is out of balance or weak
Aptitudes and talents acquired via this center appeal to entrepreneurs, heads of organizations, and corporate leaders. However, there is a catch: overuse. We drain this center when we overreach and try to force creative or mental processes on it via restless mental activity. The propensity to be forceful and arbitrary can precipitate harmful outcomes. Over-activity encourages indiscriminate and egotistic

behaviors and an imposition of one's own one-dimensional thoughts or work patterns; in this context, we push our own view no matter what (without the capacity to listen, learn, or adjust).

Exhaustion of (or deficient mastery over) this center will typically translate into stress, burnout syndrome, a lack of endurance, and a wavering mind. Corporate entities will subsequently be affected in many ways (e.g., unimaginative leadership, a lack of resourcefulness, low productivity, mediocre products, poor designs, and an absence of creativity when facing competition). Inversely, an excess of energy in this center provides for leadership that can end up in a dangerous zone, with short-term improvements that can cause destruction of certain market conditions (e.g., via monopolies). This excess can also manifest as harm to employees through exploitation, and the destruction of the surrounding social fabric and natural environments.

### Third aptitude center. Physical expression: solar plexus

"What we play is life."

**Louis Armstrong**

Adaptive intelligence fosters flexibility. The third aptitude center (*Manipur* or *Nabhi* in Sanskrit) enables the flow of change in a way that promotes evolutionary progress. In other words, the solution-oriented mind is first of all firmly rooted in its own foundation (at the level of the first center); it is equipped to act at the level of the second center; it can overcome obstacles, contradictions, and constraints via capabilities of the third center; and can finally thus arrive at a synthesis representing the best outcome for a given situation. Capabilities associated with the third center such as handling adverse conditions and managing change can help with problem-solving and crisis management.

The third center helps us win at the game of life by dealing with the tension of opposites and navigating through contradictions and choices with poise. We can map the path of a chosen future and understand our place in the chaos of a globalized yet fractured society. These capabilities provide a firm support for the individual's or organization's quest for profitability, regeneration, and dynamic equilibrium. This center rules our relationship with the material world (and the capacity to rise above it) and consequently manifests a harmonious character that enjoys serenity and peace of mind. The third center expresses itself via temperance and equanimity and is associated with an unruffled, balanced, and contented attitude. Finally, it is expressed through a sound work–life balance and sense of moderation that was the ideal of Hindu *karma yoga* (yoga of action), Confucian ethics, Greek philosophers, and Roman stoics.

Both the second and third centers are linked to the liver—the organ responsible for nourishing and sustaining the power to focus. The enhancement of human awareness via this aptitude center is expressed in several ways. Our attention, which can be characterized as the "edge" of our awareness, becomes alert and concentrated and thus favors dialectic (vs. linear) thinking. This type of elevated attention enables a greater ability to process complex data and constantly shifting conditions. Of course, making better decisions facilitates the redesign of production and of sustainability interfaces, finding one's competitive niche, new options for reinvestment, and a multitude of other positive changes in the business model.

Corporations place a higher value on resource-efficient products since a prudent use of money generates wealth. In this manner, the third center promotes the interests of businesses, in a web of checks and balances attuned to the common good of the flourishing community. There is, of course, no game without rules—rights without duties, or freedoms without laws, damage individual and organizational behaviors, as documented by the never-ending string of corporate corruption incidents. Thus, personal morals, equity issues, and CSR are best addressed at the level of the third center; located in the stomach, it carries our instinct for survival, as well as our gut feeling for right and wrong and our sense of justice. Fair play and accountability flow from this center. This focus is imperative at a time characterized to a certain extent by an erosion of trust in leadership, which can undermine the cohesion of our democracies. Citizens are fed up with politicians, and consumers often loathe corporate marketing and product manipulations.

The rules of the game are defined through a normative framework, the understanding of principles, standards, codes, guidelines, and regulatory functions. The grasp of the socio-economic context provides the rationale for balanced growth and the reduction of income inequality. The value framework of the organization is established and this defines the space of change. While rules may constrain, values always empower us and the quest for balance is ongoing. Furthermore, when corporate cultures effectively enforce self-applied ethical criteria, the need for cumbersome regulations and administrative guidelines is reduced. So, how do we internalize ethics? How can we instill ethics in a way that they can manifest *spontaneously* and in a *consistent way*?

Having is good; Being is best. Material values represent only a portion of human necessities. Thus, when we pursue wellbeing, we have to climb higher on the pyramid of needs. The game is therefore taken to another level, both more personal and more universal. We place Being above Having, a call so widespread that it is picked up today even in the slogans of mainstream politicians.

Interestingly, values are spontaneously internalized when the catalytic energy flows back from the seventh center to the third. A satisfied personality perceives true happiness (eudemonia) as a flourishing condition, and as a goal that is not simply reduced to the relentless pursuit of economic optimization. Thus, there is a balance between oneself and the other, process innovation and employment, corporate growth and ecosystem maintenance, profit and equity. Therefore, when the third center is functioning optimally, financial dealings begin to go hand in hand with nourishment and generosity.

Liberality keeps a door open for giving and one for receiving: two open doors make the air circulate and the same happens to wealth. It stimulates the circulation of knowledge, assets, and income. The flow of revenues and expenditures is kept in balance and brought back from the failed culture of indebtedness, triggering a virtuous circle of sustainability and growth. We maintain and nurture natural capital, regenerate assets, and generate value. We also invite the contributions of all those who have a stake in the wellbeing of our organizations and spontaneously aspire to co-create common value.

Opposite dimension when this aptitude is out of balance or weak
A weakness in this area of aptitude can yield myriad negative consequences (e.g., a poor learning curve, an unsteady and shifting personality, restlessness, febrile mental activity, feeling overwhelmed when confronted with challenges, inept responses to pressures, poor crisis management, corruption, and carelessness with environmental damage). Greed, impatience, a short-term vision, and miserliness indicate deficiencies at the level of this center and jeopardize the conditions associated with sustainability and enduring progress. As a result, the flow of money and resources (channeled via a focus on short-term gains) aligns with the notion that the pursuit of profit is based on the art of plundering.

Of course, "fiscal optimizations" destabilize public budgets, and abusive deregulations and the dismantling of normative frameworks contribute to the divorcing of private interests from societal goals. Also, repeated regulatory violations and a failure to conform to the current legal and social norms accelerate the criminalization of enterprises. Wealth usurpation replaces wealth creation. Thus, the entire system is corrupt when this center is shut off—we can say that the foxes are guarding the henhouse. This loss of ethics eventually leads to long-term systemic failure.

### The void (self-mastery principle). Physical expression: whole abdomen

> "The function of leadership is to create more leaders, not more followers."
>
> **Ralph Nader**

Acquisitive intelligence absorbs knowledge. Around the third center, located in the stomach, there is a zone of significance called the Void (*Bhavasagara* in Sanskrit). This center or region helps us clear the maze of illusions, prejudices, and unconscious assumptions while favoring useful learning propensities. When it is functioning well, a culture of learning enables the sustainability of success and a setback is registered as a learning episode (vs. a defeat). Here, we might consider the life of Nelson Mandela, who showed that this character trait is a bedrock of invincibility.

When the catalytic energy cleanses the Void area, we develop the capacity to be our own masters and procure proper guidance from competent and wise advisers; however, the transfer of such valuable information (e.g., know-how and artistic and intellectual wealth) often calls for educational discipline, loyalty, and esteem. Through the principle of the teacher encapsulated in the Void, where competence must inspire respect, we pass on or absorb experience; we can equip younger generations to be creative and entrepreneurial, change the world, and invent the future. We develop such abilities as moving faster on our learning curve, and even bridging the gap between opinion and knowledge, which we become willing to share.

"Having guts" is a saying that defines fortitude and self-mastery in a visceral way. The circular area that encompasses our abdomen (centered around the navel) is called a "Void" because it is void of nervous terminations; however, it is the space we need to cross in order to gain mastery (beginning with self-mastery). Interestingly, this area is also the source of our grunts when we make an effort (and exercise our will) to impose control over our bodies. However, if this area is sufficiently developed, our leadership qualities are self-evident: we are strong and resolute human beings and provide wise guidance with authority.

The principle of self-mastery, corresponding to this region, extends beyond the body's needs and into the domain of the mind. This region generates the strength to control our impulses and whims, overcome inertia, and break ingrained habits that enslave us. This area is fundamental to the development of leadership qualities. In fact, the Void might be the reason that employees follow certain leaders and not others. When this area is well developed, its competence starts to manifest as a healthy ability to lead oneself down the correct path with fortitude; others subsequently feel this at a deep level and are compelled to follow. Thus, if the self-mastery principle is strong, employees will be spontaneously inclined to follow a natural leader; however, if the quality of leadership is shown only externally (i.e., undermined by a weak Void), employees will feel this instinctively and may not follow the leader for long.

Similar to the third aptitude center, the region of the Void is also linked to our inner moral compass. We begin to feel that ethics are built-in within us rather than being driven by external laws and unwritten rules. The Void not only connects us with the inner rules of this moral compass but also gives us the strength to follow them. When the Void is infused by the catalytic energy that flows back from the seventh center, a deeper dimension of leadership manifests. Otto Scharmer (a senior Lecturer at MIT and an author of ground-breaking work on learning, leadership, and sustainability) postulates that, if someone can quiet their mind and touch their whole and authentic self, they are capable of leadership.[64] In his seminal book *Good To Great*,[65] management expert Jim Collins introduces us to the notion of Level Five leadership, which is characterized by the absence of ego and an intense professional as well as personal resolve and willpower.

When the Void is strong, a regime of applied ethics emerges automatically, without strained effort or deliberation. The thought of doing something unethical, illegal, or immoral does not even cross one's mind. Integrity and virtue flow from the personality itself.

Opposite dimension when this aptitude is nonexistent or weak
The properties of the Void blossom in a relational context: a good teacher needs a good student. However, a lack of willpower, fortitude, and a lackadaisical attitude will affect the left side of the Void (left abdomen), directly impacting the ability to lead others and perform at a good level of productivity. On the other side of the coin, being too much of a hard taskmaster—and overly enforcing strict discipline—will affect the right side of this aptitude area (e.g., employees may fear a leader and thus play along but may not necessarily follow him or her).

### Fourth aptitude center. Physical expression: cardiac plexus

The fourth center of the heart (*Riddhaya* or *Anahath* in Sanskrit) generates the courage to assert and change and the confidence to interact in a responsible and sustainable manner; it thus provides a solid micro-foundation for the creation of flourishing organizations.

Since to love is to know, it does help to be able to love oneself first. The heart center elevates our self-confidence, and helps us overcome our anxieties and become fearless; it enables us to assume our positions in the world and identify with the deeper identities of our true selves.

A welcoming house is a man's supportive biotope, the place of happiness. In Greek, *oikos* means "house." *Oikos logos* is thus the principle that rules the house and corresponds to ecology. *Oikos nomos* is the rule to manage the house and corresponds to the economy. Hence, etymology invites both ecology and economics to project a sense of belonging to and caring for our common dwellings.

The emotional intelligence of the fourth center invites us to invest in human relationships with integrity. John Mackey, co-CEO of Whole Foods, has recalled how this sensitivity contributes to the achievements of his company: "We understand so well the importance of stakeholders and the power of love in business, because they made us realize how important they were to our success."[66] The critical shift from ego to eco[67] happens through the heart. Some corporations, notably in Japan, have built their entire notion of sustainability around this sense of belonging.

Through the fourth center of the heart, we manifest the strength to protect and love our surroundings. Compassion increases the reach of love; however, it is not learned in "compassion classes" or training courses. Instead, sincerity of the heart is key. When compassion is genuine, people feel it. The one who leads from the heart inspires trust and can thus rally people and turn around difficult situations. Interpersonal bonding is established to increase the cohesion of teams, raise aspirations, and push for excellence. When employees feel valued, they respond better; corporate partners become bound in a business symbiosis by more than just shifty financial mathematics.

Thus, when the expression of such qualities is genuine, employees respond with greater motivation and strengthened dedication. As Raj Sisodia, co-founder of the Conscious Capitalism movement, has observed: "Committed employees yield committed customers."[68] The employee who is empowered is a greater asset, compared to the one who is simply controlled. The cohesion of the workforce can thus become formidable and the workplace becomes a second home for the worker.

However, the heart is not just about emotions; it is about dynamics. In the words of Confucius: "Wheresoever you go, go with all your heart." This is because the winning combination of the heart and brain, in the *ren* version of the superior administrator, delivers unmatched excellence, effectiveness, and efficiency. Furthermore, the heart vastly enlarges the cognitive range of the leader by optimizing key traits such as sensitivity and empathy. We are just a heartbeat away from a deep well of intuitions; also, benevolent guidance (vs. top-down command and control) enforces discipline and encourages human potential. A "gentler and kinder" management style signifies a capacity to lead the workforce through motivation and trust. This benevolence also expresses itself in a sense of self-esteem towards oneself—and a responsibility towards others.

When this center is fully open, we access love as energy (vs. merely emotion). This mode is of giving (vs. taking) in an unconditional, unattached way. In the independence associated with unconditional love, a sense of detachment protects our freedom of judgment from excessive sympathies or involvement. The general attitude is of greater confidence and trust. Friendship is nourishing and more real (as compared to the "likes" we may collect on our Facebook wall).

Decency, deference, and the art of respect provide, in the context of social relationships, a sort of decorum and dignity that is treasured in many world cultures and traditions. By allowing employees to be who they are, we see each other as equals and equally worthy of considerate approaches. This sense of respect is a prerequisite for establishing trust, elevating confidence levels within others, and creating true engagement among stakeholders with diverse interests, needs, and roles in the world. The force is centripetal: trust overrules centrifugal influences, overcomes racial or cultural divides, and forges lasting bonds.

Opposite dimension when this aptitude is out of balance or weak
In the absence of the deeper knowledge and balance provided by the heart, we risk pursuing a course that is disconnected from the capacity for adaptive change. Thus, without the activation of this fourth center, we can easily undermine our own course by becoming blinded by our mental projections, imposing our will and consistently mishandling the human factor.

Expressions of a dysfunctional heart center (e.g., emotional alienation, loss of connectedness, incapacity to maintain enduring relationships, affective bias, lack of courage, diffidence, insecurity, and the resulting compensation via an obsessive concern with status and reputation) are sadly prevalent these days. When the heart is closed, one lives within the walls of loneliness and insularity. An inability to relate to others affects our endeavors. Furthermore, layoffs, union busting, and the transferring of negative externalities to stakeholders are standard behaviors of "heartless" corporate leaderships.

### Fifth aptitude center. Physical expression: cervical plexus

> "The load carried together does not weigh more than a feather."
>
> **Touareg saying**

This rather complex fifth center (*Vishuddhi* in Sanskrit) is located at the bottom of the throat and controls the five senses that enable us connect to the outside world; thus, at this level, we absorb, express, and show.

Connective intelligence generates tremendous skill at handling relationships—first towards oneself and then towards social and natural environments. The mode of the fifth center is expansive and the mood is of greatness, at both individual and collective levels; the greatness of what we can accomplish manifests via this center. This aptitude brings a holistic vision and a wider capacity to identify with our natural and social surroundings, which is essential when transitioning to a flourishing organization. We relate to an entire system (which includes the corporation), have a sense of responsibility for collective action, and perceive the common good as a priority for our own wellbeing.

The fifth center is the "microcosmic operator," which expresses the distribution of the three energy flows towards the outer world. As such, it manages absorption and transfer: we take in and we release. When the catalytic energy flows through this center, we improve our social and verbal skills. Our vision gains in depth (via a process of detached witnessing) and in outward range (i.e., a bird's-eye view). The readiness to interact and project builds bridges between self and the other, in creative freedom; this is thus a principal way to channel our own energy to others. We honor our existence, express who we are, and master our language accordingly. Real self-expression is the quality of a compelling communicator whose views and visions are adopted.

To paraphrase Shakespeare, everything is theater and we perform in the play of life. As we engage in this daily performance, we recognize the difference between actor and character. Furthermore, a natural playfulness helps us to borrow roles without being fooled into losing our identities. When we understand the quiet confidence of being present within ourselves, we don't pretend or show artificial strength. In the comfort of self-respect, we are open to people and ideas, enjoy our relationships, and play the game of life with versatility.

At a first level, the properties of this eminently interactive center express through communication skills (e.g., persuasion, easiness in social and public relations, fluency, diplomacy, conflict management, and mediation). Our speech is delivered with discernment and full awareness of the listener. We make our points with a tranquil eloquence, bring people together on the same path of accomplishment, enlarge the audience, and achieve a goal. Critical negotiation skills are optimized and cooperative partnerships strengthen the corporation.

The support and enjoyment of collective processes can open new horizons. As we overcome the narrowness of perspectives often associated with individualistic approaches, the ensuing solidarity can promote a group's long-term effectiveness. A strong team-building propensity (awakened by the heart) can thus be applied to maximize the efficiency of management and also the productivity of the workforce.

The capacity to join the meditative state, at the deeper level of this center, manifests when energy flows back to it from the seventh center in the limbic area of the brain. Then the fifth center facilitates detachment from results and enjoyment of the process. A balanced mixing of heart and head raises our alertness beyond reactivity. Observation from the central witnessing platform, without outside manipulation or influence, can yield a visionary dimension. The strategic vision is focused, the goal is clear, and policymaking gains in pertinence.

Through this witnessing state, we can better comprehend the web of interactions between all stakeholders, the goals of the company, and the needs of society. Our antennae pick up more signals. Senior management listens to the opinions of others and recognizes the best advice. After the power of the heart is awakened, the emotional quality of trust brings collective action to a new level of effectiveness. This is how "leaders understand the fine art of building trust."[69]

Connected leaders can comprehend the interactions between economic actors, societies, and the environment. For example, they prioritize the importance of ecosystem services for business survival and promote new ranges of products and models—priming business sustainability. When integrated approaches are enacted together within business cycles, they bring greater structural stabilities to the market. When we understand the interdependencies and feedback loops associated with our organizational systems, we realize that "working with nature is more productive than working against it."[70]

When we consider the dire assessments from recent Intergovernmental Panel on Climate Change (IPCC) reports, it is clear that reaching this vast horizon of sustainability is a necessity for corporations that seek to stay ahead of the curve given the climatic projections for the next century. A healthy, overarching balance between profitability and a commitment to humankind promotes the advent of a global, sustainable economy. Thus, sustainability is based on understanding and adapting our role within an integrated spiritual, cultural, and socio-economic ecosystem.

In conclusion, the capacity to evolve on the central channel is associated with the capacity to master bipolarity via the witness state. When we witness the world as well as ourselves through the skills of introspection, we do not justify our mistakes and are capable of self-correction and progress via a rapid learning curve. Introspection and a witnessing capacity reveal and dissolve the "unconscious bias." We don't fool ourselves, need to fool others, withdraw, or become aggressive. Our speech is under our command. We develop a "contextual awareness" of the whole and know how to integrate our thoughts and actions and customize our products for the market.

When we shift "from ego to eco," we focus more on collective organisms vs. our individual self-interest. Moreover, when energy returns from the seventh center to this fifth "microcosmic operator," contextual awareness turns into collective consciousness, connective intelligence becomes a reflex action, and a portion of the information within our relational world becomes instantly and spontaneously integrated. However, we must strive to achieve a healthy balance between individual freedom and collective wellbeing.

Opposite dimension when this aptitude is out of balance or weak
When this center is out of balance, a capacity to convince is lacking. Jealousy undermines necessary bonding and teamwork. Actions based on guilt and diffidence can impede our abilities to take a stand, sufficiently defend corporate interests, and take necessary (but difficult) ethical positions. Furthermore, when we keep our heads in the sand, we accumulate wrong turns and lost opportunities; also, posturing and pretensions will often signify shallowness, while aggressiveness can generate misunderstandings, activate polarity (vs. consensus), and provoke conflicts and antagonistic responses.

Misjudging the ecological, economic, or competitive environment causes an inadequate allocation of assets; this floods the market with inadequate or unsafe products. Business models, associated with a lack of oversight, focus on the bottom line; thus, the process of making and selling products can lead to excess capacity, environmental costs, and waste. Some of the gravest expressions of the malfunction of this center are reckless disregard for public safety, water wars, pollution hazards, habitat destruction, and associated species extinction; however, when this center is functioning well, it promotes our sense of responsibility towards the common good.

### Sixth aptitude center. Physical expression: optical thalamus

> "Do not make yourself so big, you are not so small."
>
> **Jewish proverb**

The sixth aptitude center (*Agnya* in Sanskrit) is located in the center of the head and manages our brain and awareness.

The blood–brain barrier is a selective physiological permeability barrier that separates the circulating blood in the brain from the extracellular fluid in the central nervous system, and prevents the entry of neurotoxins or other pathogens that could hamper crucial neural functions in the brain. We can use this example as an allegory to explain the barrier function of the sixth center.

It works a bit like a locking mechanism at the subtler level of our inner consciousness mechanism to prevent disturbances from emotions or thoughts, desires or volition, in order to enable the state of higher thoughtless awareness in the seventh center. Indeed, only the attention carried by the rising subtler catalytic energy can pierce through this constricted gate. In that sense, meditation practitioners or seekers of this higher state who use mind concentration or mental power usually find themselves riddled with the unwanted side effects of such exercises: sleeplessness, irritability, panic attacks, neuroses, etc.

In other words, the goal is to be able to reach beyond mental activity whenever we wish; however, this is not obvious to those of us who are actively using the mind. To do so, we need a certain level of

control over our own thought processes. However, do we control our thoughts or do they control us? Can I stop thinking if I wish to?
Unlikely.

The space of thought is like a dense asteroid field that the searching vessel of the attention cannot pass through. Most of us cannot cross the thought barrier. The sixth center is the secret passage through this field, a subtle junction at which a cognitive parting takes place between opinions and knowledge, delusion and truth, between being alienated and facing reality while assuming ownership. The catalytic energy is ultimately the only power which, rising by itself through the central channel, can cross the hidden gate of this constricted space. Crossing this passage represents a defining moment: we are about to break through into another plane of awareness, the Great Seventh center situated at the top of the head, where we achieve a paradigm shift in our consciousness which enables the manifestation of our highest potential.

This breaking-through by the catalytic energy is not a consequence of mental concentration or mindfulness. The opening of the passage between two thoughts interrupts the incessant rise and fall of thoughts and introduces us to a space of silence (*vilamba*) in the mind. Peter Senge, senior lecturer at the MIT Sloan School of Management and founder of the Society for Organizational Learning, focuses on the need to suspend our thinking and see our seeing.[71] In a sense, we renounce our thoughts with their constant bombardment which tends to take over our attention. Like the spectator of a movie who is no longer taken by the screen or immersed in it, we become the spectator of the screen, of our thoughts. We do not surrender to them, but we surrender them to our inner silence. This process helps to increase the space between two consecutive thoughts.

Subsequently, our penetrating intelligence pierces the mental fog. We can enter into the gap thus created and live in the peace of the present moment—a pleasant experience of calm freedom which offers new possibilities in "the power of now." With sharper clarity, we go beyond the mindset of trade-offs, simply perceive things as they are, and avoid misdiagnosing situations. Thus, we can better face life; in fact, we can cut through layers of appearances, the maze of issues and options, and we can sort out mixed messages. Successful transformation is guided by the avoidance of parallel projections, mental concepts, or virtual realities. The transparency we achieve in our perception washes away doubts and fears. The act of letting go of such heavy luggage brings lightness and freedom.

At this level of an open sixth center, we experience the liberating feeling associated with the capacity to forgive many types of transgressions such as pettiness, sarcasm, slander, jealousy—to name a few. The psychological impact of being aggressed is overcome by the power of forgiveness. When we forgive, we are subsequently protected by thicker skin. We do not react; we move on. Forgiveness is priceless; it is perhaps the most important weapon we can wield in our quest for inner peace.

Freedom supports innovation; we do not need to follow the herd. The elevated awareness enabled by the sixth center helps us to "see outside of the box"—thus, the Eastern reference to a third eye. We exit the obscurity of Plato's cave, the noisy box of concepts, and we can sharpen the aptitude of the fifth center. This type of perspective also combines the visualization of longer-term consequences of present business decisions and the capacity to evaluate alternative courses of action. Thus, managers identify opportunities and risks and become better equipped to lead their organizations towards a flourishing state.

As we cut through prejudices, acquired habits, and conditionings, a strengthened faith in ourselves emerges. This space also enables us to receive eye-opening intuitions. This subsequently allows us to accomplish much more than through our usual analytical efforts. Canadian journalist, bestselling author, and speaker Malcolm Gladwell urges the investigation of the "power of thinking without thinking."[72]

Of course, the quantity of information is never a substitute for the quality of knowledge. A subcenter called *hamsa* in Sanskrit—located between the eyebrows—helps guide our sense of discernment. It functions as a navigational device, works in symbiosis with the fifth and sixth centers, and functions as an inner radar. As "the discriminator," the *hamsa* is a key mechanism for learning adaptive change.

This subcenter activates discerning intelligence that enables good judgment, convincing prioritization, accurate risk assessment, effective differentiation (of right from wrong), and greater decisiveness in decision-making. Since we know what we are doing, we know when to insist and when to let go.

Opposite dimension when this aptitude is out of balance or weak
Vanity is a waste of identity. When we attempt to "market" a virtual personality, we confuse others—and ourselves. Furthermore, when we are overtly influenced by the views of others—or stubbornly impose our own views on them—we judge the true state of affairs poorly. We can thus contribute to an oppressive workplace via pettiness on one side and egotistical and/or delusional behaviors on the other. Weak judgments, an inability to prioritize, indiscriminate choices, and poor decision-making undermine results. The inertia of incumbency yields lackluster leadership.

For instance, in a business context, marketing relies too often on undercover manipulations (e.g., of images, tastes, statements, and desires), which can sometimes promote artificial or harmful lifestyles. Thus, supply-side manipulations distort a rational allocation of resources (associated with the welfare of consumers and longer-term interests of society). Also, vanity-based sections of the marketing industry (e.g., the luxury sector) can invite us to build phony images and virtual identities. This takes us off a mainstream path where we can determine real needs and deploy real solutions.

\* \* \*

In this chapter, we have explored the four types of energy (left SNS, right SNS, PNS, and catalytic), the way they affect our moods, temperaments, and thoughts, and how they affect our attitudes and actions. We also looked at six out of the seven aptitude centers and their qualities (and opposite dimensions). While they are innately present in these energy centers and nervous plexuses, they tend to manifest at varying degrees in each individual.

Once the catalytic energy is awakened, it flows through the aptitude centers and their aspects are spontaneously awakened. This has major implications—at both personal and organizational levels. Individuals no longer have to strive to attain certain qualities (e.g., self-discipline, ethical behaviors, forgiveness, dynamism, and focused attention); they become "automatically" enabled and manifest effortlessly in day-to-day activities.

This turns the traditional paradigm of training on its head. As opposed to trying to develop such qualities via external learning and repetitive exercises (until they become second-nature), they can first become established within individuals via the flourishing of their aptitude centers. This occurs as the flow of catalytic energy increases and subsequently starts expressing itself in daily life—at work and at home. In fact, we were surprised to hear from individuals who attended our meditation sessions and benefited from the aforementioned processes; they told us that they not only became better employees over time but also better parents, spouses, and managers.

We now proceed to address the seventh and last center. We have dedicated an entire chapter to it due to its paramount importance. The reason the seventh center is critical is because it represents the gateway to a new dimension of human awareness—collective consciousness—through which sustainability-as-flourishing manifests through our thoughts, feelings, and actions.

# 5
# The field of collective consciousness

"Meditation is not something we need to learn; it is something we need to discover."

**Center for Evolutionary Learning**

Can the expansion of our awareness reach a collective level? Can an integrative cognitive capability then manifest and yield decisions and actions that are directed towards the common good? How do we know whether a given meditation technique is actually helpful? We must admit that—to the best of our knowledge— as of this writing there are no rigorously defined "quality control protocols" on meditation, its effectiveness, or the potential side effects of specific techniques. Thus, the validation of our hypothesis (i.e., spontaneous meditation, based on thoughtless awareness, can lead to a sustainable transformation at the individual and organizational level) rests on the experiences of trainees who were rigorously monitored and analyzed.

Is contemplation strictly passivity or is it action within inaction? Is meditation shutting off inside or expanding the mind with greater clarity and insight? We submit that the deepest stage of meditation is the opposite of concentration: it is letting go, crossing the gate into the silence of inner peace and opening the window for intuition. We refer to meditation as an inner state of deep integration of one's own awareness with the reality of the present moment, which is devoid of thoughts that bombard us from the past and future and beyond merely attaining relaxation and wellbeing. Over time, the awakened catalytic energy increasingly activates the inner qualities of the aptitude centers and elevates the value systems of meditators—thus enabling them to reach their full potential. In addition, meditators become "collectively conscious," which refers to the ability to tangibly perceive the state of their own and others' aptitude centers and energy flows, use their own catalytic energy to correct any imbalances thus perceived, and develop an integrative awareness of the "whole" (e.g., organization, society, and environment). This is reflected in decisions and actions that are geared towards the common good. In other words, our inner computer becomes connected to the network.

This type of tangible perception manifests as a sensation of gentle coolness that can be felt at the top of the head and in the palms—after the catalytic energy is awakened and pierces the seventh center. Thus, the awakening of this energy is not a mental or theoretical construct; it is an actual happening that can be felt objectively on the physical level. Coolness and other types of sensations are felt on the palms, which are like maps of our energetic systems. Over time, the practitioner thus becomes able to diagnose—and subsequently correct—imbalances in the aptitude centers by directing the catalytic energy towards the required areas. (A detailed description of these meditation techniques is beyond the scope of this book.)

The (PNS-based) spontaneous meditation described in this book can give access to this new dimension of consciousness. This is due to the fact that it is not dependent on the SNS but rather accesses our reserve power (i.e., the catalytic energy). We can meditate simply because meditation is already a part of us; it is not something we need to learn; rather, something we need to discover.

In the previous chapter, we described the first six aptitude centers with a summary presentation of their properties. These are human qualities that we all possess to varying degrees, which is why we can so easily identify them; however, when the values or qualities of the aptitude centers are integrated, the impact is much greater than the mere sum of the individual properties of each center. However, in many individuals, these properties are most often *not* integrated.

This is where the seventh center comes into play.

The seventh center is located on the top of the head (the fontanel bone, which is soft in infants) and corresponds to the limbic area of the brain where a multitude of nerves converge like spokes of a wheel. These nerves come from all parts of our nervous systems (i.e., left SNS, right SNS, PNS, and all nervous plexuses, which are the physical manifestations of the aptitude centers)—thus integrating in this apex region of the brain all the properties described in the previous chapter. A synthesis takes place between emotions and thoughts, love and knowledge, and the qualities of all the aptitude centers. Thus, the seventh center plays a key role in taking the leap towards collective consciousness due to this capacity to integrate, which we will describe shortly. Baffling as it is, the immersion in this new consciousness happens very simply and spontaneously.

## The world, the mirror, and me

French philosopher and anthropologist Claude Levi-Strauss (1908–2009) was one of the central figures in the structuralist school of thought. Mindful that we are living on a planet increasingly at risk, he affirmed that we need to change the course of history—a feat much more difficult than changing the course of ideas.

Today, many in the scientific community agree on the importance of changing the system to address climate change and the host of other organizational and societal issues we face today. Many are still struggling, however, to figure out exactly *how* to change ourselves in order to change the system. How do we translate the value components of our ethical standards into natural and spontaneous behaviors? In other words, how do we get to "true North," where decisions and actions for the good of the whole are automatic and effortless? The impelling factor is the present business climate which forces us to focus on answering some of these key questions.

Let us illustrate how we might get there. The biological and adaptive function of aesthetics has contributed to the success of *Homo sapiens*, according to Dalhia W. Zaidel, a researcher in behavioral neuroscience at the University of California, Los Angeles (UCLA).[73] This has brought the human tribe together by providing a standard of shared knowledge. Semir Zeki, a neurobiologist who pioneers neuroaesthetics research at the University College London (UCL), proposes that the structure behind the shape of our universe is reflected in the organization of our brain. Thus, in the aesthetic experience, the brain exhibits the mirror effect (i.e., its functioning reflects the mechanics of the universe).

Recent research into neuroaesthetics suggests that the same area of the brain (Zone A1 of the median cortex orbitofrontal) is activated by the (external) experience of perceptions of beauty and the (internal) experience of self-absorption. Thus, it is as if "inside" and "outside" are two relative terms and, when in a condition of connectivity, our consciousness stretches naturally from the individual to the collective dimension. The functioning of the brain via a "mirror effect" seems a lot like a scientific corroboration of Plato's notion of *episteme* (i.e., the brain experiencing knowledge as a capacity to perceive things as they are and recognize what is true), which is rejected by relativist philosophers. Thus, it is intriguing (and almost poetic) that NASA seems to have recently identified a correlation between a vibrating sound sent by the sun and an ancient sacred sound that Hindus identified as the *Aum* mantra.

Still, a reflected image is only as good as its associated mirror. Furthermore, our own imperfections will create imperfections in the way we perceive a more abstract reality. (In the concrete world, consider how our ability to read letters on a distant sign depends on the quality of our eyesight.) Thus, our ability to use a new faculty of cognition to perceive a subtler reality (e.g., the energy flows and aptitude centers of ourselves and others) would depend on the "clarity" of our instrument of perception (i.e., energetic channels and centers). The health of this subtle system cannot be taken for granted; it has been likely affected (positively or negatively) by the various episodes that occurred throughout our lives. Fortunately, there are also techniques for improving our inner instruments via specific meditation practices, which have been verified over several decades by myriad practitioners across the world.

The mirror can be perfected.

Carl Jung spoke of the commonality found in the depths of the psyches of all individuals: "The deeper 'layers' of the psyche lose their individual uniqueness as they retreat farther and farther ... 'Lower down', that is to say as they approach the autonomous functional systems, they become increasingly collective until they are universalized."[74]

As a further elaboration on Jung's psychological explorations of collective consciousness,[75] we submit that the collective consciousness is this mirror. Specifically, it is supported by the central nervous system as the catalytic energy rises up the spine and reaches the seventh center. The "mirror" in our brain enables us to perceive the collective (i.e., others and the "whole") and to experience, on our central nervous system, the fact that we are an integral part of a whole. This new awareness then influences our actions and decisions for the betterment of the whole (which also includes ourselves). If this aptitude (i.e., the "brain as the mirror") can be actualized in business leaders, it will empower them to

> **An encounter with Shri Mataji Nirmala Devi (1923–2011)**
>
> The authors of this book chose an empirical path, undergoing personal defining moments and convincing experiences, before embarking on the daunting task of sharing this knowledge for the benefit of entrepreneurial economics. More fortunate perhaps than Gurdjieff in his "meetings with remarkable men,"* they recall their encounters with an extraordinary woman. In August 1975, one of the authors met Shri Mataji Nirmala Devi in England. By the time he landed on the doorstep of her home in Hurst Green, Sussex, he had already traveled many paths in his young life; however, he was not prepared for what he was about to discover.
>
> The lady of the house was affable and welcoming; she offered a cup of Indian "chai" and revealed herself to be an amazing cook. A very uncommon spiritual master, she was attentive, spoke to the point, and conducted a sort of "soul therapy." Shri Mataji was at →
>
> \* Gurdjieff, G., *Meetings with Remarkable Men*. Martino Fine Books, 2010.

ease with the subtler intricacies of ontology and cosmology, and her penetrating knowledge was oriented towards the visitor—a self-described common man, loaded with his own burdens and limitations. Her psychological perspicacity carried a desire to comfort, counsel, and heal. Through a number of sessions of guided meditation and "chakra workshops," she awakened his catalytic energy: the *Kundalini*.

After a number of days and many such sessions, a cool breeze emitted from the fontanel bone at the top of his head during a meditation. *"You've got it!"* she exclaimed happily.

This condition was intimate in its obviousness and the direct sensation of physical and psychological wellbeing could simply not be missed, ignored, or denied.

In the words of the fortunate visitor:[†]

> *Far from the auto-hypnotic attempts or psychic manipulations that I had witnessed previously, this experience was permeated by the joy of a higher reality, the reality. I* ➡

[†] De Kalbermatten, G., *The Third Advent*. New York: Daisy America, 2003: 158.

acquire a clearer picture as well as improve their capacities to know where, and on what, to place their focus.

Still, the above presentation of our subtle network of aptitude centers and energy flows is not yet complete. Balancing the left and right SNS and coming to the central path of the PNS is necessary; however, it is not sufficient for delivering full connectivity with oneself and the world and attaining a flourishing state—individually and collectively. In order to realize our fullest potential, we must enter the area of "the Great Seventh" aptitude center.

Explorations— in various philosophies, world cultures, and traditions—into the perfectibility of man and our higher cognitive potential have revealed diverse references to this seventh aptitude. For example, this apex center has been known as the thousand-petalled lotus in Buddhist lore (due to the large number of nerves converging in the limbic area of the brain) or manifesting as tongues of flames on the heads of the apostles. Indeed, this is also where the paths of spirituality, science, and direct perception come together.

The Great Seventh is the most complex of all centers. It represents the culmination of all our capabilities and is the instrument that can enable a

## The "great seventh" aptitude center. Physical expression: limbic area

Over the past few decades, a number of meditation methodologies (mindfulness, concentration, visualization, and other related techniques aimed primarily at relaxation and wellbeing) have captured the media's attention to varying degrees. For the most part, they activate the SNS (left and right sympathetic nervous system) and deal with the concentration or observation of the mind, emotions, mental intensity, or some type of focused and repetitive activity, reaching only up to the sixth center. We submit that a simple meditation system, based on the activation of the catalytic energy, helps us to discover the psychosomatic underpinnings and potential of our cognitive systems. The existence of the seventh center (*Sahasrara* in Sanskrit) may not have been suspected by 18th- and 19th-century rationalist thought systems; however, there are explicit references to this inner instrument in several world cultures and medical practices. The age-old metaphor of rebirth, expressing

higher level of empathic connectivity (i.e., the "collective consciousness").

> *came to understand that Shri Mataji had introduced me to that state of consciousness of Samadhi where existence, bliss and truth melt in one integrated and glorious condition of being.*
>
> The following day, during a train ride to Victoria Station and subsequent walk through London, he had such a feeling of lightness that he was checking whether his feet were even touching the ground. The quality of sight and silence, of easy serenity and wellbeing, was astounding. He also enjoyed a sense of proximity to, and empathy with, other living beings—as if this new consciousness had a collective dimension.
>
> Shri Mataji explained why the unconceivable was suddenly available: the much-sought-after jump into the fourth dimension of spontaneous meditation was simply corresponding to the evolution potential associated with the present phase of human history. Thus, far from considering it a miracle, she invited her students to consider this game-changing step as a natural process in the growth of consciousness. They were the owners of this potential; they could, themselves, become catalysts to share this experience.
> →

With much humor and simplicity, she loved to emphasize that evolutionary leaps—significant as they may be—are quite natural. And, while they had also taken place in the past, this new one was registered in the human consciousness.

Having this experience of self-realization is a gentle happening that mostly registers as a cool breeze ("vibrations") and a serene, enjoyable lightness in the head. However, it contains, at its core, the wonderful sensation of being completely and absolutely real. Furthermore, in some rare instances, it can also be quite powerful.

> The vibrations coming from her increased and felt cooler, but soon my attention was taken by another dimension. The top of my head was coming alive and I had the sense of it opening, and I felt like the outpouring of an incredible liquid awareness. I became drenched in an inner lake of joy, which then coagulated into something that I can only described as a solidified state of bliss. My eyes were closed and gradually, slowly, the cup overflowed and the bliss started flowing down from my head into my whole ➙

something that happens by itself to our consciousness, carries an understanding of the elusive nature of the seventh center; however, this does not prevent us from clarifying the implications of a process that depends on the PNS. Such a method of meditation is, by definition, beyond the reach of our desire (left SNS) or willpower (right SNS) and cannot be achieved by our own efforts.

We now accept that chimpanzees, orangutans, elephants, and dolphins react in ways that could be interpreted as self-recognition, which places them ahead of other animals in their learning capacities. Similarly, the specific phenomenon of consciousness in human beings is susceptible to growth and adaptation when meeting biological purposes, such as the evolution of the species.

Abraham Maslow, among many, has identified the contribution of self-actualizing individuals.[76]

We have seen in Chapter 3 that various parts of the brain sustain the stream of consciousness, being responsible for generating conscious experiences. Some of these neural correlates[77] bind together information in a manner that integrates various types of experiences that are both sensory and internally generated. This direction yields further clues that are associated with the empowerment of the brain.

When the ascending catalytic energy enters the limbic area, it integrates and reinforces an extensive connectivity between parts of the brain that deal with perceptions of the inner and outer world. This flow of energy also has a healing effect and further reveals (and integrates) the aptitudes of the centers previously described via a direct cognition based on the workings of the central nervous system. These properties, which are integrated in the brain, manifest and combine in instant synchronicity.

With this coordination at the level of the brain, the properties stored in the six lower centers can now be tapped into through spontaneous meditation—via the medium of the catalytic energy (which "connects" them like a thread passing through seven pearls). In the same way that the colors of the rainbow are integrated into white, the properties of the aptitude centers are integrated in the silence of thoughtless awareness. While the state of thoughtless awareness is normally very difficult to attain and sustain, it is made possible (and developed over time) by the "awakened" limbic area of the brain which has been stimulated by the catalytic energy.

> *body, filling every nerve. It was both a state and a sensation, both spiritual and physical. O my God! I could not even utter these words; but I was just the awareness beyond the words. It was a flow, a river of beatitude; something that literally and completely, in the parlance of the time, blew my mind. What I had known of the intensity of physical love seemed only a tiny inkling, a spark of this.‡*
>
> The most shocking dimension of this experience was how real it was: evident, immediate, and complete. This confirmation—that the brain was able to experience so much more than known before—was startling in its obviousness. The brain had opened its hidden treasure chambers without ingesting drugs or other chemical boosts.
>
> The full narrative of this encounter—including its implications—has been published elsewhere; however, it suffices here to remark that Shri Mataji also explicitly saw, in this transformational experience, a beneficial way to empower entrepreneurs and other economic and social actors.
>
> ‡ De Kalbermatten, *op.cit.*: 161

Such properties are elusive and hard to measure; however, ongoing research offers new evidence for old theories. The seventh center is about the engineering of neural systems—and the integration mechanism beyond the limits of the controlled mind. Holistic intelligence is essentially integrative; furthermore, it is our observation that ancient philosophies, cognitive neurosciences, and the evolutionary record of our species appear to increasingly combine into a new effort—the exploration of the promise of consciousness experienced at this integrative level of the seventh center.

Below this peak center we try and strive. But up here we close the uncertainty gap and enter an all-new comfort zone: we succeed without trying; our action bears fruits effortlessly, without particular intent. We spontaneously unfold all the aptitudes needed to address virtually any situation. We enter a state of "not doing" (*Wu Wei* in Chinese, *Sahaja* in Sanskrit) and nevertheless accomplishing. We emanate a charisma that convincingly attracts. We are consecrated with the trust and loyalty of others.

Leaders burdened with considerable responsibilities develop tendencies to fix things—as a matter of fact, to fix *everything*. In the linearity of this habit, we may fix what isn't broken or make matters worse. Thus, the awakening of the limbic area greatly helps us to sense when to act and when to let go, when to fix something and when to go with the flow. For example, some important battles were won because victorious commanders resisted the impulse to charge too early (e.g., Hannibal vs. the Romans in Cannae), while others were won by avoiding battles altogether (e.g., Kutuzov vs. Napoleon in Russia). Thus, there is action to be found within inaction.

"Don't react; just see!" was one of the insightful advices given by Shri Mataji Nirmala Devi. We watch in silence to reach beyond the asteroid barrier of the movement of our thoughts. On the screen of awareness we watch the comets of emotions. We watch facts and absorb better their informational content that is relevant for our purpose. We see in serene gratitude how things work out by themselves. Our state spontaneously expands into a pleasant relaxation, away from deliberation and the attempts to concentrate the mind. All the while, of course, we still use the power of thought, analysis, and deduction, when we choose to do so, rather than being dominated by their constant chatter.

This is all driven by the activation of the PNS via the awakening of the catalytic energy, which is then sustained and nourished through the practice of thoughtless awareness. Meditation is also medication, as the additional energy that we are able to absorb in the absence of thoughts triggers a self-healing, psychosomatic process. The energy is then supplied from the seventh center downwards—moving through the different aptitude centers and restoring their health from any earlier damage. This restorative supply flows through the parasympathetic portion of the central nervous system. The inner system goes into "detox" mode and a kind of "psychic immune system" lends renewed resilience to the personality.

Spontaneous meditation intensifies the connectivity between the different parts of the brain. The brain can sustain our talents by opening connections between the neural cells. This self-feeding positive psychology carries holistic intelligence that brings us within the reach of *Wu Wei* (non-doing) and into the domain of serendipity.

The relationship between each aptitude center and the seventh center helps to manifest the respective properties and expand their impact. For example, the second center provides the energy necessary for thinking, planning, and other forward-looking mental processes, as well as fresh dynamism and spontaneous creativity (vs. mentally derived knowledge that is forced or "squeezed" out of a fatigued brain) via the highest mode of operation associated with the seventh center. Insights reveal themselves as pure inspiration—and seemingly out of nowhere. Furthermore, the ability to "go beyond reason" signifies not being unreasonable, but rather being in a mental state that is devoid of acrobatic mental computations. In this area of the brain, the best rhyme comes spontaneously to the poet, the right inspiration to the novelist, the insight of discovery to the scientist—and the vision to the true leader.

When the catalytic energy moves back from the seventh to the sixth center, it yields greater clarity of perception and depth of intuition. A flow from the seventh to the fourth center of the heart enables love to be experienced in a fuller, more joy-giving way; furthermore, existence itself becomes more enjoyable and the unhappy consciousness dissolves. Gratification is experienced as a flowing "zone of grace"—a state of being that carries us well beyond the satisfaction of ego pampering or material remuneration.

How does it work?

A key aspect of the system of spontaneous meditation is the activation of the catalytic energy. This phenomenon provides access to the fourth state of consciousness[78] in the limbic area and thoughtless awareness gradually yields the spontaneous manifestation and integration of the best aspects of human behavior (e.g., creativity, accountability, satisfaction, benevolence, courage, loyalty, cooperation, solidarity, discrimination, insight, self-mastery, and so on). Such capacities are already activated to varying degrees in the members of today's corporations and administrations; however, the subtle impact of their integration has largely been lacking. The application of just one "stand-alone" aptitude overlooks the benefit of combining them (e.g., the added value of integration, connectivity, and serendipity conferred by the seventh center); the whole can truly be greater than the sum of the parts. Thus, integration can bring a *qualitative change* to the manifestation of each capacity (for instance, the combined aptitudes of the Void and the sixth center provide for visionary leadership, which goes beyond the individual qualities of either the Void area or the sixth center).

Under the hypothesis we are presenting, this form of "seeing" in contemplation (thoughtless awareness) is not only a state of the brain but also a state of the entire body with all its seven aptitude centers and three energy flows. We have mentioned that medical research has investigated the impact of spontaneous meditation on our autonomous functions such as, for example, lowering blood pressure. Meditation can also impact the way our genes work, as it has the ability to activate (or deactivate) portions of the DNA genetic code.

Meditation changes the way we produce biochemical substances (i.e., it can modify stimuli and the built-in reward system). Since our reasons for doing things change accordingly, meditation enlightens decision-making. Far from causing a withdrawal from the mundane world, the balancing of the sympathetic and parasympathetic systems brings the best of both worlds (conscious vs. unconscious, action vs. inaction). Such people, in the words of the master Kuang Tzu, become sages in their placidity and kings in their activity.[79]

The unconscious competence of the limbic area of the brain integrates all aspects of our being and takes us to the core of who we are. This is why it can sustain and nourish all of the aforementioned energies, capacities, and aptitudes: the virtues of our hidden potential manifest. This is the breakthrough of consciousness: emotional and thought processes dissolve into the direct perception enabled by the newly wired central nervous system.

Occurrences, at this level, cannot be scripted; thus, they are fresh from the source, genuine, and leave mind-training focus far behind. In the freedom of this condition, we move forward effortlessly on the path of inner and external achievements. Serendipity orchestrates, with surprising ease, a ballet of places, moments, and circumstances to generate ideal outcomes. The groundbreaking French scientist Louis Pasteur wondered: "Did you ever observe to whom the accidents happen? Chance favors only the prepared mind." This is because the integration of the brain's neural network enhances connectivity with the outer world.

One of the most stunning properties of the opening of the Great Seventh is called "vibratory awareness." This refers to the capacity to register with our central nervous system (i.e., via physical sensations) the subtle state of our inner being, of others, and of the environment (the above-mentioned sensation of coolness felt in the palms and above the head is one example of such sensations). Thus, vibratory awareness works like a ground-penetrating radar; it can pick up variations in the condition of the psyche of an individual. This is a little like magnetometry: a technique used in archeology to reveal special features or anomalies under the surface of the soil.

Therefore, *know thyself* and *know others* is no longer an irreconcilable paradox associated with theory of the mind. In an evolutionary explanation of consciousness, a deepening of self-knowledge goes hand in hand with an ability to recognize and empathize with the inner states of others. We no longer do everything with only the volition of the conscious mind. In fact, a combination of unconscious and conscious competences gives an immense comparative advantage when we attempt to interpret and anticipate behaviors. When leaders can combine both competences harmoniously, they can lead their organizations to greater competitive advantage.

The deeper empathy that binds us thus becomes manifest[80]—as a perception that makes us conscious of the entire biosphere. Solidarity and eco-awareness become spontaneous. Capitalism and community become compatible; the ensuing wealth is also distributed. Thus, empathy can effectively be shared, if not taught, by meditation.

In *A Whole New Mind*,[81] Daniel Pink cites empathy as one of the key dimensions of a new conceptual age. However, the type of empathy we are referring to is not a psychological aptitude or an emotional projection; instead, it is an expanded consciousness that can perceive others and the whole—a phenomenon that has been explored in the writings of leading French thinkers, such as Henri Bergson and Theilard de Chardin. This is key because collective consciousness can yield new-found political, economic, and social efficiencies, where business leaders will need to claim their ground. Improved business management evolves organically and appears to fall into place in a graceful and natural movement. The application of this ultimate aptitude at the organizational level is described in Chapter 6 as the M-shaped corporation.

The state of non-duality (*Advaita*) corresponding to the seventh center—in which the *knower* and the *known* merge in the act of *knowing*—has long been described in ancient Sanskrit treatises. However, this subject matter has remained esoteric and out of reach because the associated toolkit was missing. Furthermore, the path to this state was arduous and very few who tried, ascetics and other seekers of a deeper reality, were able to achieve it. However, the opening of the seventh center was invariably associated with an exquisite quality of the enjoyment of non-duality (*Advaita Bhogini*). Some of the finest minds have, at times, described the elusive experience of the seventh center via expressions that seem to defy everyday understanding (e.g., "joy in action," "love as energy," "beatitude," "enlightenment," "self-realization," "doubtless awareness," and "meta knowledge"). Psychologists have developed their own definitions.

With more enjoyment and less stress, professional achievement and the enhancement of wellbeing converge. Indeed, the last center in the limbic area of our brain manufactures chemicals such as dopamine and serotonin which are responsible for engendering happiness and gratification. As meditation takes our awareness to this center, we gradually learn to synthesize higher levels of wellness. In this context, the limbic system (which is connected to both rational thinking and emotional experience) mixes and matches information that reaches our brains via a new reward–punishment mechanism. Our contentment does not only stem from the activation of external stimuli; in fact, we can attain significantly better control over the scale of expectations and rewards.

We may thus finally establish the neural foundations of sustainable ethics: "doing the right thing" is not imposed by the law or social norms but it is now encoded in the brain's rewards circuitry through a change in brain activity. We simply express an inner adherence to ethics, in the same way we take, for instance, to aesthetics. This is because acting ethically provides a higher satisfaction. Doing the right thing becomes more enjoyable.

Life after meditation is the same ... and yet very different. The unbearable lightness of being fades away, displaced by a new-found gravity of being that is indeed most enjoyable to bear. Life at the level of the seventh center provides fertile ground for the maintenance of an ever-adaptive evolution. In this sense, we can claim that the collective consciousness capability sustains the very conditions for sustainability.

These experiences of "becoming" have been researched. In fact, there are references of such states of being in various cultural traditions. Our research in the field of meditation is supported by cross-cultural references that point to the notion that such states are within the reach of all those who seek them.

The simplicity of the above-described condition is sometimes referred to as wholesomeness, unity, universality, oneness, or fulfillment. The integrating properties within the neural network of the brain can bring higher states loosely captured in notions such as plenitude of being, liberation, blissful vacuity, or complete freedom.

We do not need ecstasy pills to reach *nirvana* because, fundamentally, the satisfaction of a higher level of consciousness comes with merging into our innermost state. The opening of the Great Seventh center brings us closer to superior lucidity.

When the seventh center is closed (which is the standard condition of *Homo sapiens* caged within the elastic walls of thoughts and emotions), the corresponding aptitudes of immediate perception, spontaneous synthesis, and integrative knowledge are naturally nonexistent or weak. This is why the failings and shortcomings related to the previous centers—as described in Chapter 4—feel quite familiar. We have no other way, beyond uncharted religious beliefs, to trust the guiding evolutionary force that propels everything forward.

Of course, individuals are frequently entrepreneurs, decision-makers, and businesspeople; however, we lead businesses (and not vice versa). In other words, the dimension of an accomplished leader in any field of human activity will depend on his or her associated personality traits. However, there is a hidden and intriguing symbiotic relationship between individual and corporate transformation. In the next chapter, we will submit the hypothesis that one can decipher how the psychology of an enterprise reflects the ruling trends of its administrators and leaders. We contend that human organizations project their own psyches, on a par with living organisms. Thus, would it not be to the advantage of managers to become more conscious of this?

We have now reached the level of the argument where we must move from the instrument (*yantra*) and technique (*tantra*) of individual flourishing to the more collective level of corporate flourishing. We will first explore some of the archetypes that shape not only flourishing individuals but also the life and progress of organizations.

# Part III
# Towards the Flourishing Organization

# 6

# The transition models of organizations

"Business knowledge is the knowledge of creating wealth out of nothing—like an artist does."

### Shri Mataji Nirmala Devi Srivastava

Is the concept of a "flourishing corporation" just wishful thinking?

Of course, it is impossible to thoroughly consider the issues associated with corporate change when we focus on symptoms as opposed to root causes. For instance, many business leaders simply hope for positive market fluctuations to make their problems disappear; unions rarely encourage financial responsibility because they fear that benefits will be cut; politicians are often afraid to annoy voters or instigate social conflicts and associated citizen-led initiatives, such as seeking to dissuade investors from owning shares in companies that work against the public good.

A flourishing corporation which rewards itself, its customers, and society as a whole can be expected to be less affected by such trends. But can "flourishing" be benchmarked by indicators measuring participatory decision-making, sustainable territorial development, green energy, and quality biological products? Or is this all about ethical investing, environmental, social, and governance (ESG) reporting, and CSR? Surveys have indicated that there is a mildly positive correlation between the pursuit of socially responsible policies and financial returns. In some cases, firms with high ESG ratings have outperformed the market as a whole. However, is the force and speed of this trend sufficient to generate required systemic changes—even as the planet is heating up? Skeptics, today, remain correct when they respond in the negative.

Outside pressure on corporations can work; however, it generally does not work well and fast enough (e.g., institutional investors are unlikely to be persuaded to divest by activist campaigns and the records of big polluters generally show that their performances remain unaffected by such pressures).

Flourishing corporations are firstly sustained by the enlightened individuals guiding them. Clarity, in the context of this type of integrated consciousness, depends on the condition of the aptitude centers within each member of the organization. In order to handle the decoding of these sensations (e.g., on the fingertips), we learn to absorb more "know what" and "know how." Empowered entrepreneurs, decision-makers, and collaborators spread the benefits of a more holistic cognitive mastery (and its associated benefits) on associated groups, products, suppliers, and customers. However, this must all start "at home," i.e., within.

## Spelling the alphabet of corporate transition

### The M-model of corporate evolution towards the enlightened organization

In this chapter, we will show how the promise of Proposition 2 can be fulfilled:

> ***Proposition 2: Organizational evolution.*** *The diffusion of sustainability-oriented decisions and actions by individuals and small groups can be supported by strategic, operating, and cultural change*[82] *initiatives undertaken by an organization. This would generate a virtuous cycle of bottom-up and top-down stimuli and responses, resulting in profound*

## 6 THE TRANSITION MODELS OF ORGANIZATIONS

> *changes in the purpose, identity, and mission of the organization—towards the creation and expansion of the common good for all stakeholders who contribute to it.*

Prominent thinker and author Arie de Geus contends that organizations can be meaningfully compared to living beings: "Everything the company does is rooted in two main hypotheses [. . .]: (1) The company is a living being. (2) The decisions for action made by this living being result from a learning process."[83] If each of us has an inner network (as described in previous chapters), complete with bioenergies that flow and affect our tendencies to act in one way or another, would it be possible that such individual tendencies and associated energies can manifest at a group level as well? These correlations would be intriguing. For example, we have hinted in Chapter 4 how the complementarity of the first two energies of the triple flow model will engender a perpetual instability. Interestingly, it seems that the market is unable to escape this pattern[84]—and the same is true for the corporation.

Of course, there have been countless public discussions focused on the need for radical changes in the way business is done; however, they most often reveal how helpless we all are in terms of suggesting suitable ways out. This puts the focus on *managing* sustainability issues rather than addressing deeper organizational problems at the root cause. Of course, the discourse on sustainability needs to be shifted towards healing the environment and our societies (vs. sustaining unacceptable conditions). Still, a consensus among many authors dealing with CSR and sustainability is that individuals must change first—before lasting changes can be successfully implemented.

We have so far submitted that changing our individual ways is a first—and very necessary—step; however, how we can bring these changes to an organizational level? Furthermore, what would a flourishing institution look like? This chapter illustrates how the triple flow model applies to an organization.

## The corporate U

Many of the problems of corporate action, in the modern world, are linked to a duality in business processes characterized by pendulum movements between two extremes: *productive* and *administrative* processes.[85]

### Productive processes

These processes are short-term and future-oriented dynamic actions corresponding to the right SNS as described in Chapter 4. They represent the driving force of action in the corporation. These actions are based on creativity, (will)power and discipline, and are reflected in production, services, R&D, innovation, strategy, and sales. Productive processes represent the core of a corporation's business model where products or services are developed, produced, and sold. They include practical and technical aspects of operation and production, design processes, and services. Such actions are carefully planned, sequenced, and measured and the associated skills are highly regarded.

Resources are allocated in accordance with the needs of production processes. The front office drives the charge. While there is a tendency to acquire more, move faster, and always need more, restrictions (e.g., legal and administrative) set limits—even when higher degrees of freedom might be demanded. Thus, under such pressures, there is temptation to cut corners and take significant risks. Such behaviors are justified by the need for growth and profit maximization, which are considered key measures of organizational strength. Cutting-edge technological innovations will also often turbocharge associated productive processes.

Success is generally measured in strength and power within the organization and its associated market, social, and political environments. Power is mostly expressed in financial and material terms such as *profit, shareholder value, capital, salary,* and *status symbols* (e.g., the architecture of company buildings, office location and size, and company cars and clothes). Behaviors, associated with these processes, can be characterized by the cultural dimension of *Masculinity* as introduced by Geert Hofstede.[86] Internal myths and legends worship extreme action (e.g., non-stop work across consecutive days to achieve a critical goal), high risks (e.g., taking on and fulfilling a lucrative contract without the necessary capacity), or domination and acquisition (e.g., driving a competitor out of business). Aggressiveness is seen as a positive (and even necessary) trait for doing business.

## Administrative processes

By contrast, such processes are based on past experiences, knowledge, traditions, habits, culture, and conditionings that correspond to the left SNS as described in Chapter 4. Administrative processes are handled mainly via corporate support functions (e.g., accounting, finance, HR, IT, and facility management). They are an expression of a desire to sustain the overall organization. Actions, in this domain, are based on caution and protection. Standardization and regulations are designed to keep up with a status quo and based on well-structured processes and a framework that enables them to be safe and productive. There is high regard for both internal (e.g., codes of conduct, organizational rules and procedures) as well as external (e.g., legal and financial regulations) knowledge.

Administrative-related resources are deemed essential for securing the company's existence. Associated organizational actions are regulated via a complex web of protocols and bureaucratic rules. Also, the power of administration is measured by its ability to keep up an existing structure; however, in extreme cases, bureaucracy can get entangled in its own web. The result can be a passive attitude towards action and change—and a reduction in the speed of business change which has to adjust to the slower tempos of bureaucracy. At this point, slyness may be confused with good administrative conduct—and stagnation with a state of balance. Myths and legends may internally develop in association with efforts to push through new regulations, successfully protect the organization against change, or take control of a large budget.

However, well-functioning administrative processes can keep the corporate machine well oiled, organize the caring for corporate stakeholders, and the compliance of the organization with external regulations.

## The pendulum

Both productive and administrative processes ensure the sustenance of an organization. They flow into two separate channels (i.e., the right and left SNS, respectively). All actions of a corporation occur in an area between the two extremes of action orientation and bureaucracy; the movement of a pendulum, associated with such corporate actions, will reflect the various degrees of such tendencies and follow a path that resembles the lower section of the letter U.

**FIGURE 11. Pendulum swing of corporate actions**

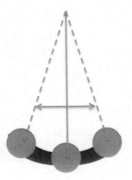

**FIGURE 12. Basic poles of corporate action**

An organizational state close to equilibrium can be maintained as long as there is a steady pace between the growth of productive processes and administration. Evidently, however, such a state is not highly stable; for example, too much emphasis on productive processes (L-shape) or administration (J-shape) can cause imbalances, which eventually can cause a whole organization to lean to one side or the other. When a firm starts to distinctly favor one side, the effects will be felt within its environment and by its stakeholders. As the firm looks for support to stop this tilting movement, it will lean on something (e.g., the natural environment) or someone (e.g., stakeholders) and extract as many resources as possible in an effort to regain its balance. As the imbalance becomes more extreme, it will look for support wherever it can get it and can thus potentially crush other structures which will give in under the strain.

**FIGURE 13.** L-shape tilting towards production

**FIGURE 14.** J-shape tilting towards administration

## The L-shaped organization

A domination of production processes represents the classical model of predatory capitalism, which is oriented towards profit maximization at any cost. The L-shaped organization seeks to suppress administrative processes that slow it down and strives for maximum independence from all limiting factors (restrictive legal regulations, taxation laws, the influence of unions, NGOs, etc.)

When an organization tilts too strongly in this direction, the inbuilt aggression affects internal and external stakeholders. The negative consequences can include environmental effects (e.g., pollution, other waste, and the maximum use of "free" resources, such as water and air), the domination and exploitation of employees (e.g., erosion of labor standards and abusive layoffs), ruthlessness towards suppliers (via financial suffocation) and customers (via unhealthy products), and a loss of social responsibility (e.g., withdrawal from solidarity through fiscal optimization). Ultimately, an entire society and culture can be affected by the establishment of unethical behavior patterns and the stimulation of destructive or addictive tendencies.

In such situations, greed prevails over ethics and humanism—on individual and collective levels. Furthermore, the organizational culture of an L-shaped company rewards aggression and the use of power to attain frequently unrealistic profit goals; examples of this type of organization include Enron, Arthur Andersen, and Lehman Brothers. Of course, this is not to say that today's institutions are devoid of such excesses.

## The J-shaped organization

If an administration dominates processes within an organization, it may initially limit (and ultimately potentially strangle) productive processes. Organizational power, associated with this type of administration, strives towards a high degree of dependence—nothing is supposed to move within the company without the consent of the administration. Of course, this can lead to disproportionate growth of administrative functions and an overwhelming number of bureaucratic processes.

J-shaped companies lose touch with their original organizational purpose (e.g., production, service, and agriculture), fail to adapt, become unproductive, and can ultimately destroy themselves. In order to survive and sustain an expensive (and potentially overburdening) administration, these companies often depend on external support such as subsidies. The self-protective nature of such an administration leads to behaviors and attitudes that would favor the failure of an organization over accepting a reduction of power (such as when Nokia clung to its product and past achievements and missed a key product evolution in their market segment). We see similar acquired reflexes in the world of politics.

Any significant, lateral tilting movement of an L- or J-shaped organization causes a crisis. While timely and well-controlled counteractions can lead to a new quasi-equilibrium, late and/or inadequately strong or weak counteraction can cause the whole organization to wobble for a while—with an unsure result. A lack of (or delayed) counter-actions will cause the whole institution to fall to one side or the other—resulting in the elimination of the existing structure and a likely end of the organization.

In the absence of an immediate crisis, the illusion of equilibrium may be generated for a while; however, it is never really sustainable. Still, organizational development can be characterized by quasi-equilibrium—when only minimal action is needed to stabilize the whole. While this is the best type of scenario for corporate managers, it should not be confused with a true state of balance. Quasi-equilibrium is simply the absence of major shakes in either direction, resulting in a "blurry U" and constant interactions between the two poles (e.g., numerous little movements between the left and right and a continued transfer of stress and tensions to societies and stakeholders). Many business leaders see this condition as "normal"; in fact, the idea of attaining any other form of equilibrium would be considered utopian.

In order to attain true balance, organizations need to evolve.

## Advancing beyond the great (economic) illusion

A new level of organizational development can only be attained once the great economic illusion of a "growth only" focus on shareholder value (and profit maximization) is overcome. The realities of a salient focus on growth (as a dominating economic principle) have been widely explored and include destructive effects on societies (e.g., poverty, child labor, and destruction of family structures), environments (e.g., climate change, deforestation, poisoning of water, and loss of soil fertility), and economies (e.g., financial crises and financially destabilized governments). The pressure to produce profit sometimes pushes industry sectors (e.g., manufacturing, healthcare, food, and pharmaceuticals) to promote practices (e.g., planned obsolescence) and products that can work against consumer interests. However, they can still be perceived as promising remedies for preventing small- and large-scale economic crises, despite the relatively widespread awareness that the boundaries that restrict them exist for the benefit of our planet (ecosystems) and our society (ethics).

This "economic illusion" refers to the pendulum motion between the two extremes of left (administrative) and right (production). The problems it engenders push corporations to search for ways to (i) redefine their purposes in a sustainable way, (ii) arrive at a new definition of corporate performance, and (iii) establish a culture oriented towards the satisfaction of all stakeholder needs. However, such change can only be successful if the mindsets of all actors (e.g., owners, managers, and employees) change.

In order to attain this objective and reach a new level of awareness (at the individual and collective level), a new evolutionary pathway must be opened, as described in earlier chapters. This needs to start at the individual level before it can scale up to the level of the organization.

As we have seen in the previous chapters, the individual in search of personal balance can experience this personal transformation via the flow of the catalytic energy which awakens the qualities of the seven aptitude centers. This facilitates personal advancement through a balance between desire and thought, commitment, and detachment—towards the realization of one's full potential.

One acquires the ability to see through the mist of illusions via the expansion of one's personal capacity to stay balanced, sense, learn, and transform. This improved clarity goes along with an ability to anticipate, integrate, and make the right choices at the right times—in a spontaneous manner. These are critical qualities for transformational processes—and doing business in general. For a manager who activates the qualities of the aforementioned aptitude enters, this means that he or she becomes able to play the economic game in a new and more effective way. At the same time, the door for innovation and adaptation (of even the most centralized corporate processes) is opened: an energy flow has started, which works for the evolutionary ascent of the corporation.

## The W-shaped organization

Individuals thus enabled, in the right positions, can significantly help transform fruitless and extreme organizational pendulum swings by profoundly redirecting the energy of the swing into collective ascent and growth (as opposed to directing it towards one of the two extremes). Action on either side of the U now becomes channeled in an upward, central movement, which is needed to move the entire organization out of the pit of seesaw linear policies that ultimately lead to destructive acts. Of course, corporate change will not happen as swiftly as on the individual level; however, it can be implemented at a collective level via the motivation of dedicated and transformed individuals.

This change process is similar to what Otto Scharmer described in his Theory U.[87] Specifically, individuals sense the need and opportunity for transformation, seek change and presence (by letting go of old patterns) and invite and accept intuition and inspiration. Thus, they effect evolutionary actions by prototyping or enacting nascent ways that can eventually be institutionalized. This realization and integration of new processes is similar to what Scharmer describes in his theory; however, the actual personal transformation (which is supported by the catalytic energy flow that leads to an expanded consciousness) goes beyond *Presencing* (as we shall explain shortly when introducing the M-shaped corporation).[88] The change will be initiated by many small but significant changes in the individual's corporate microcosm and will ultimately follow the principle of leading by example (regardless of the level in the organization).

If a critical mass of managers and employees has internalized this personal and organizational transformation and has commenced to introduce appropriate changes in their spheres of the organization, a push of support for collective change through the use of the catalytic energy can be expected. Additional dynamics then become available to fuel change and innovation. Building on the increased individual and collective capabilities, new ways for organizational development and evolution along a third stream of action (as opposed to only the two extremes of the left and the right) can be found and implemented.

This third channel is established in the center of an organization and functions like a stabilizing pole, which provides additional support to the structure. When production and administration are led by inspired individuals, when they stop working against each other and begin to contribute to the growth of this new stream of actions, the organization's overall energy pattern changes. Various functions start to support the new balance, strengthen the overall organization—and help realize its full potential (vs. being pulled into different directions and fighting for attention and power). Thus transformed, the original U changes into a W. This introduces the triple flow model—with an added central channel to provide true balance (vs. an unstable quasi-equilibrium between pendulum swings).

**FIGURE 15.** Original U-shape

**FIGURE 16.** Stabilizing the central channel

This transformation furthers organizational clarity (i.e., a consensus on how processes are to be handled in order to be universally beneficial) and strengthens the expression of aptitude centers that are translated into sought-after business aptitudes (e.g., stability, wisdom, creativity, temperance, fairness, courage, dignity, humanity, trust, vision—to name a few). The aforementioned aptitude centers are, of course, located along the central channel. Thus, through this redirection of energy flows inside an organization, a new stability is attained; the energies of the former U are now balanced and support the whole in a constructive way, as opposed to constantly being pulled in different directions. The productive processes generate balanced growth via creative innovation; also, wealth is created in and around the organization, and stakeholder interests become embedded in such strategies. The administrative processes ensure stability, secure the sustainability of organizational processes, and assume the role of nourishing and nurturing internal and external stakeholders.

Thus, the previous U-shape oscillations between the L- and J-shape phases of an organization evolve into a new phase (W-shape) representing the "good" corporation with increased stability and a much firmer command of its resources and interactions.

**FIGURE 17.** W-shaped organization aiming for connection with the surrounding collective consciousness

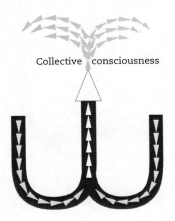

Through an improved connection to social, ecological, and economic environments, corporate processes will more naturally consider the needs of the company's stakeholders. At this stage, the company has evolved to become a good citizen—as well as a socially responsible and environmentally conscious one. In other words, the third stage of a corporation (captured via the W-shape) fulfills the promises of Proposition 2.

Still, how can management maximize the chances for a "good" (i.e., W-shaped) corporation to become truly successful as a flourishing corporation?

## Realizing full potential: the M-shaped organization

The most intriguing proposition of this chapter is the subtle but important distinction between the W- and M-shapes—and the submission that the M-shape (flourishing) corporation can exist at all. We understand that the reader, at this stage, might not outright accept this proposition and thus merely consider it as a hypothesis.

In the W-shaped company, an inner enabled ascent generates the deployment and alignment of corporate resources. This focused movement surpasses the immediate limits of U-shaped organizations such as opposing tensions and a self-centered organizational awareness. However, more can be achieved. We have seen that, through the opening of the seventh aptitude center, a critical threshold is being crossed. Activating the aptitudes of all centers in a more integrated manner represents a qualitative leap of consciousness. This breakthrough step can also happen within an organization when a critical mass of progress on the central channel has been achieved.

The finality of the transformation along the central channel must be explained. With the activation of the central force of the triple flow model, the old patterns of the J- and L-shapes contained in the U, which are still reflected (in an improved manner) in the W-model, will be transformed as well. When this phase is reached, the W-shaped firm shifts and transforms into an M-shaped corporation, the characteristics of which are as follows.

In the M-shape, new stimuli affect corporate strategies. Objectives are now derived from greater swaths of knowledge and are thus far-reaching. The focus of corporate activities shifts from balancing the duality of production and administration towards a capacity to absorb and process knowledge from a newly integrated cognitive system (i.e., the collective consciousness as previously described). At this stage, corporate processes are integrated and more effectively interlinked. Furthermore, the central pillar of the M is enlarged by an expanded capacity for connectivity and integrated absorption (which correspond to the faculties of the seventh center). The seventh aptitude center, atop this central pillar, serves as a synthesis node and functions in a way as a central distribution station for the energy and information flowing through the corporation. Through this gateway, the information and energy exchanges enabled by collective consciousness now support and effortlessly align all processes within the organization.

**FIGURE 18.** M-shaped organization: enlightened, enriched, and energized feedback

In the M-shaped organization, the manifestation of all aptitudes of the seven centers happens in an integrated and effortless way and informs all actions and behaviors. Whereas previous change programs based on new measures, policies, and other top-down or bottom-up initiatives may have failed in the same organization, the M-shaped corporation now possesses those qualities *intrinsically*, which is why they manifest spontaneously in daily life. The inner magnetic field of the organization has changed; the compass of the corporation is now pointing to true North, and there is no longer a need to try to force it into a given direction.

The overarching aptitudes of connectivity and integration establish a link with the collective consciousness of which we are all a part. All learning and insights acquired consciously or unconsciously during the evolution of the organization are transmitted into this collective consciousness. The manifestation of this learning will be fed back into the processes of production and administration via this significantly expanded awareness. This will result in an increasing synchronicity in thoughts, feelings, and actions. These dimensions—expanded beyond open hearts, minds, and wills—complete the vision of Otto Scharmer.

This feedback flow will reflect not only what was put originally into the collective awareness by the organization and its members, but will also capture the enriched signals from the larger collective unconscious beyond the corporation which can be remarkably potent. Through this cycle of energy flows connecting the organization and its individuals with its environment, closer understanding and interactions are established and reinforced, benefiting all stakeholders of the company as well as the organization itself.

The result is a drastic expansion of the boundaries of the company—leading to true inclusion and integration on all (corporate and societal) levels. The company is not only serving its stakeholders and doing charity work, it is also naturally realizing its place in society and on the planet. Thus, it will work with its stakeholders via a new relationship that is no longer characterized by power games but by genuine mutual interest and cooperation that are inherent in the organization. As the true North of the compass is now built into the DNA of the company, doing the right thing is almost automatic, effortless, and spontaneous.

We would, of course, not submit the M-shape hypothesis without also providing an iterative process for its verification; however, accessing these vastly expanded capabilities requires a certain level of corporate preparedness. To this end, the type of experimentation-based learning process described in Proposition 2 can help the company attain its flourishing best. Such a process contains a collective recognition of the renewed purpose of the organization, which transcends agenda-based interests and aims to bring 360-degree benevolence for all stakeholders.

Inspiration and intuition in the state of serendipity (i.e., in the flow of collective consciousness) will often become determining patterns for action and decision-making across entire organizations. Some processes will change. For example, energy-sapping, forward-looking mental elaborations and planning processes, originally part of productive actions of an organization, will be reshaped to have greater reliance on insights, creativity, and inspiration (vs. mentally derived knowledge) under the impact of expanded connectivity and better integrated faculties, which will be centrally provided within the organization.

The energy of an organization is composed of the energies of its members. The "weight" of each individual energetic contribution is in a direct relationship with the rank and influence of that individual within the group. A right-sided, action-oriented leader can only compensate so much for a left-sided, lackadaisical group; similarly, a dynamic, right-sided organization can be hindered, to a certain extent, by lethargic, left-sided leaders. Balance can be attained in a W-shaped corporation if there is an awareness of the two extremes and a desire and ability to bring balance towards the central pillar. If both leaders and employees are unaware of the corporate slant and everyone moves towards the same extreme (i.e., lethargy on the left or hyperactivity on the right), the organizational shift will be accentuated—away from the central energy flow and towards the L-shaped or J-shaped corporate transition models.

A flourishing (M-shaped) corporation is characterized by three powerful capabilities: (i) *awareness* (ability to perceive deviations from the central pillar), (ii) *self-correction* (ability to address its self-diagnosed deviations and bring them back towards the center), and (iii) *connectivity* (with the stakeholder ecosystem). These capabilities must be expressed at the level of the individual (in leaders as well as employees) in order to effectively work at the level of the organization—and subsequently the society and the environment—via the collective social impact created by a critical mass of M-shaped corporations.

In this chapter, we explored how the triple energy flow model of individuals translates into the evolutionary patterns of organizations. We looked at the U-shaped pendulum between production and administration and the imbalanced states (L and J) it can promote (which correspond to the right and left sides, respectively, of our sympathetic nervous system). We also delved into a third state of corporate evolution (i.e., the W-shape), which can bring the L and J back into balance via the addition of the central energy flow. Finally, we took a peek into the future, which is represented by the flourishing or enlightened organization: the M-shaped corporation.

# 7
# Practical steps for the transition

This chapter is designed to provide practical steps to chart the journey towards the flourishing organization, illustrated through the examples of two companies with very different cultural dispositions.

Interventions in organizations always work on both the individual and the organizational level in parallel, since change in the individual represents the nucleus of deep organizational change. Some organizational changes have been leveraged by interventions on the individual level alone, and such results can be impressive—particularly if the individual is positioned at a reasonably high level in the organization. However, as mentioned in Chapter 2, in order for the organization to flourish, it is critical that the individuals composing it achieve *and sustain* a flourishing state over the long term.

In order to achieve lasting and substantial organizational change, we deem the following dual approach to be more all-inclusive and robust:

1. **Sustainable development**

    The introduction of conventional change interventions that increase sustainable business practices following the triple-bottom-line[89] approach throughout the company. These changes need to take place on all core levels.

150  THE EVOLUTIONARY LEAP

FIGURE 19. The double helix model (of transition towards the flourishing organization)

Sustainable Development →

**7. Integration and collective shift towards the Flourishing Organization**
Collective consciousness and integration of both evolutionary strands in all processes and structures

**6. Identity and cultural change**
Embedding system-level thinking in the DNA of the organization

**5. Structural change**
Align governance structures

**4. Stakeholder integration**
Including stakeholders in decision-making processes

**3. Testing change interventions**
Interventions towards CSR and sustainability in pilot studies

**2. Development of strategies**
Strategic roadmaps on organizational and unit levels

**1. Diagnosis**
Assessing overall disposition in terms of L-shape or J-shape, as well as mindsets, values, business processes and practices

**7. System-level consciousness**
Awareness of interdependencies among actors in the system

**6. New system of values**
Internalized flourishing of responsible and virtuous values

**5. Embedding meditative practices**
Reflective and meditative processes in day-to-day business practices

**4. Diffusion in the organization**
In different departments and units

**3. Introducing meditative practices**
Individually and/or in groups

← Reflective Development

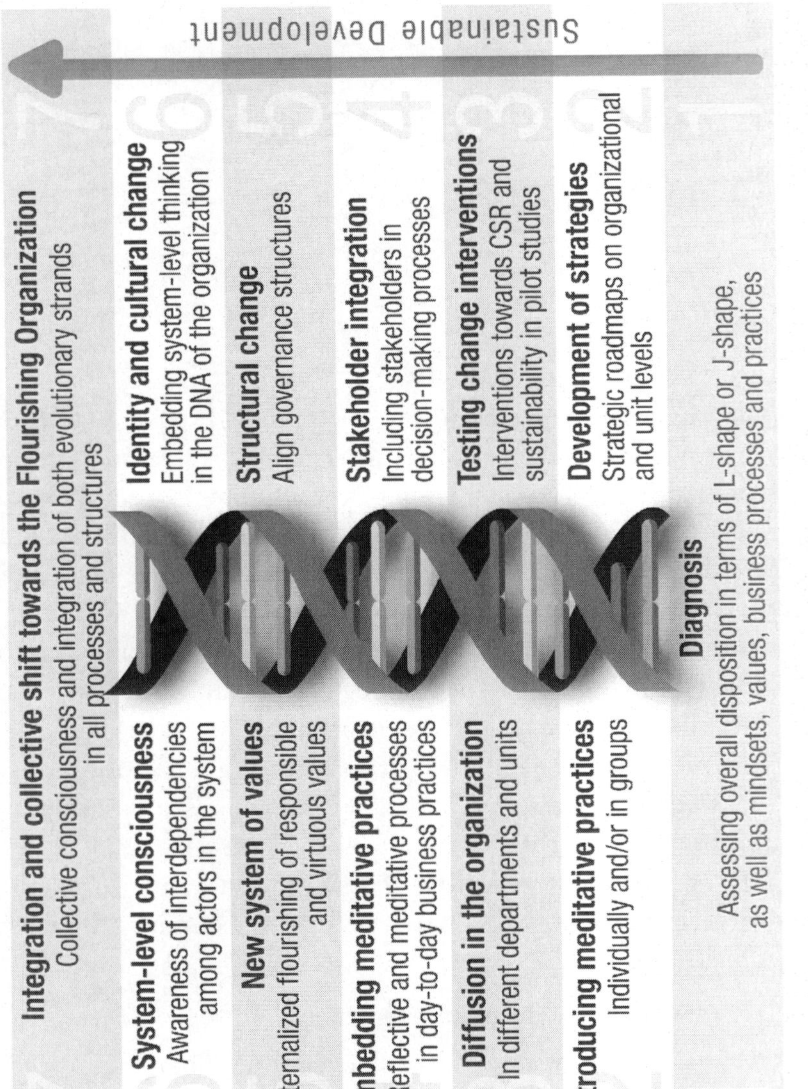

2. **Reflective development**

> The embedding of reflective and meditative practices in business processes (involving internal as well as external stakeholders) both on the individual and organizational level. These practices are not necessarily focused directly on business aspects in all cases, but rather on the individual and team aptitudes required for the corporation to flourish.

At the corporate level, the evolution of the whole organization requires a mix of conventional change initiatives and reflective and meditative processes—on a par with how conventional medicine addresses specific needs while alternative medicine focuses holistically on body and spirit resilience and the strength of the immune system. In an integrative medicine approach, traditional Western medicine may still be required (e.g., for combating infection, reducing very high fever, or removing a tumor); however, deeper healing will raise the level of preparedness of the body for a lasting recovery. Interestingly, it is essentially the same with organizations—an evolutionary leap is more likely to happen when symptoms of imbalance are removed along with a concurrent introduction of a more holistic management culture.

Change developments—associated with reflective and sustainability processes—take place in parallel and support and enhance each other. They involve the following steps:

## A. Reflective development

1. **Diagnosis**

    Assessment on this level focuses on the identification of the L- or J-shape disposition of the company and individual value structures. This is similar to the step we described as "Know Thyself" in Chapter 2 (i.e., individual development); however, it now refers to the organizational level.

2. **The introduction of meditative practices**

    Meditative and introspective practices (individually or in groups) are introduced in different departments and units on various hierarchical levels. The results on the individual level will be monitored and assessed regularly to assist with individual flourishing and mastery.

3. **Diffusion in the organization**

    Successful programs will be offered in different parts of the organization—and at different hierarchical levels—to develop nuclei of meditators who can extend the positive effects throughout the organization. These groups will gradually start to develop new perspectives and express them within the work context. This will increase the collective awareness within the organization.

4. **Embedding meditative practices**

    Building on the developments in previous steps, reflective and meditative processes will be introduced in the internal business practices and processes: for example, the introduction of balancing practices in conflict situations or as a focusing exercise at the beginning of meetings. These practices will open new ways to perceive business challenges and lead to new strategies to tackle these challenges.

5. **New system of values**

    As the examples in Chapter 2 illustrate, the expansion of meditative practices in many organizational areas will have an effect on the value structures of employees. The further these reflective practices spread, the more the overall value structure of the company will change—responsible, virtuous values will initiate collective internal flourishing. This is a process that flows on its own and has to be allowed, or witnessed, rather than managed.

## 6. System-level consciousness

At this stage, the organization will have attained a much greater awareness of developments in its environment and the interdependencies among actors in the entire ecosystem. This form of organizational empathy will enable the firm to better perceive and anticipate the needs of its stakeholders and the impact of its own actions on its social and environmental ecosystems. At this level, the company will have developed a significantly greater stability and will use this new position to introduce business models that reflect this new understanding. This stage can only be attained if the company's leaders lend their full support to this development.

## 7. Integration and collective shift towards flourishing

A shift in the organizational awareness level will enable the integration of new behavioral and mental patterns in all areas of the business. Together with the development on the organizational sustainability front, a stable balance will be attained and substantial changes in business processes can be gradually introduced. Eventually, this will lead to the establishment of an M-shape corporation that has evolved through all seven stages of reflective and sustainable development. In the M-shaped organization, achievements at the lower levels are the rule rather than the exception, and this new culture will be defended against any regressive tendencies which may try to reverse this development.

## B. Sustainable development

### 1. Diagnosis

Diagnosis at this level focuses on assessing (i) sustainability mindsets in employees, (ii) sustainability strategies, and (iii) business practices.

2. **Development of strategies**

   Based on the diagnosis from the previous step, corporate sustainability strategies (and the sub-strategies of departments and business units) will be evaluated and transformed into sustainability roadmaps at various levels. The integration of these roadmaps will provide a strong basis for the sustainable development of the organization at all levels.

3a. **Testing change interventions**

   Based on the aforementioned strategies, this step includes the development of interventions that are associated with CSR and sustainability (economically, socially, and ecologically). In pilot projects, these interventions will be attempted in settings that enable pre- and post-assessments (to ensure rigorous measurements of the impacts).

3b. **Internal diffusion**

   The interventions with the best impact will be selected to be diffused throughout the organization and constantly improved. In this process, stakeholders will be engaged in strengthening the impact and outreach of the selected initiatives.

4. **Stakeholder integration**

   Collaboration with stakeholders will be further intensified. This will enable the organization to receive support for new sustainability strategies and business models via internal and external sources that will gradually be included in collective decision-making processes.

5. **Structural change**

   The above-mentioned strategic changes must be reflected at structural and governance levels in order to be most effective. Necessary adaptations to organizational structure will be introduced with increasing speed to support new patterns of leadership and decision-making.

6. **Identity and cultural change**

    Cultural change will uniquely manifest into new ways of managing the business via the integration of sustainable and meditative principles. System-level thinking will become deeply embedded within the DNA of the organization. This will be reflected in the self-perception and boundaries of the organization and will mark the attainment of the W state.

7. **Integration and collective shift towards the flourishing organization**

    Ultimately, the organization will reflect its identity and expression in the role it plays in society and in the ways it conducts business. Thus, reflections on the purpose of the firm, particularly via meditative practices, become a powerful activity and signify further enhancements to the enterprise model over time which positively impact all internal and external stakeholders.

This type of organizational development represents an evolutionary process; thus, precise step-by-step milestones and timeline horizons cannot be predicted in detail beforehand. We anticipate that the first, second, and third steps, in both strands of the helix depicted in Figure 19, may take between 12 and 18 months. The fourth, fifth, and sixth steps can be expected to take another 12 months—and will eventually lead to the flourishing organization.

Naturally, this type of deep transformational process will likely face some criticism and certain obstacles (e.g., the opposition of managers and employees who do not appreciate introspective processes, or negative feedback that may be received from certain stakeholders). However, this fact-based approach can be introduced in accordance with the associated capacities of employees and other stakeholders. Thus, challenges can be addressed and dealt with at the appropriate speed—without halting the overall evolution of the organization.

As described in Chapter 2, several portions of the proposed process have been implemented in various corporate contexts and have shown encouraging results. Although this process has yet to be fully attempted within a single corporation over a sustained period of time, we will now illustrate a potential implementation via two examples of (partly fictional) companies that represent L- and J-shaped organizations. While some of the steps described in the double-helix diagram have yet to be tested (particularly beyond Step 5 within both strands of the helix), many implementation examples are inspired by actual experiences from corporate programs we have conducted. The associated feedback from participants is based on real quotes, although the names have been changed.

## Example 1: ALPHA Corporation (L-shape)

Founded in 2010, this U.S.-based wholesaler and online seller of outdoor sports equipment and fashion became a very successful business. By 2016, the company had more than 350 employees and $100 million in annual revenues. Nearly 90% of its products were produced in Asia. Sixty-five per cent of the managers were male.

### ALPHA step A1: Diagnosis

ALPHA Corporation showed a strong L-shape, indicating an action-oriented company with a culture revolving around power and dynamism; management hierarchies were flat. Economic success was the highest goal. Due to its rapid growth, ALPHA's resources were often stretched. Seventy-plus-hour workweeks were the norm for employees in management positions. Internal communications were rather aggressive. Overworked and stressed employees and team leaders were often caught in the crossfire of conflicts; not surprisingly, attrition was high despite competitive salary levels. Due to chronic time crunches, decisions were often made ad hoc, without following due process. Management decisions often involved significant risks. One of the founders said that ALPHA's motto was "Business is an extreme sport!" Furthermore, following the administrative processes were considered unprofessional in the context of the company's culture, and sales and marketing strategies were pronouncedly aggressive.

Despite the appearance of growth and strength, internal dysfunction inhibited effective teamwork and prompted the company's leadership to seek our advice on how to improve business processes. In order to bring the organization into balance and move it from its overbearing L-shape towards stability and sustainability, we recommended the following interventions:

- Provide structure for the business processes (i.e., shift away from uncoordinated, aggressive, ad hoc styles of management)
- Reduce stress and tensions between employees
- Reduce the tendency towards precipitated, overly aggressive action
- Introduce socially responsible mindsets
- Integrate and align corporate processes
- Strengthen team structures
- Increase awareness of stakeholder needs

## ALPHA step A2: Introduction of meditative practices

Report 1: Introduction of stress management programs

In our interventions, the introduction of voluntary, free-of-charge stress management sessions is usually one of the first steps. At ALPHA, the offer to join weekly meditation-based stress management sessions was offered to a few select teams via an internal online newsletter and through communications from team leaders in staff meetings. The first meditation group was rather small, heterogeneous and included members from the sales and marketing team, the head of packing, two administrative assistants, and an HR manager.

The meditation group grew rapidly size in the following weeks, when word of its positive results spread through informal channels. Bob Harrison, the head of packing who used to be feared for his temper and harsh comments, became visibly calmer and less reactive—much to the delight of the packing department. After two months, three meditation groups were running on different days of the week with an average of seven to eight participants in each group.

No business topics were discussed during the meditation programs. The focus was solely on inner balance and introspection. Most participants experienced deep relaxation in the sessions, attained the state of thoughtless awareness, and started to practice meditation techniques to prepare for stressful meetings or situations; many also began to practice at home in order to strengthen their experiences. Thus, they were able to use their awakened catalytic energy to not only balance themselves but also to help bring balance to teams.

Below is some initial feedback provided by participants:

> **Reports by meditators**
>
> "Wow, this was great! Just using the different affirmations and working to let go of the associated daily stress felt wonderful and freeing."
>
> "Honestly I was a little skeptical. I did not think that meditation would have such significant impact (and in such a short time) on my complete personality. This experience surprised me positively. I did not think it would produce such a significant change. These four weeks have completely reversed my initial skepticism. I am completely satisfied and would like to continue."
>
> "I think I found a way to find serenity in moments of stress and exhaustion. Such profound moments are not easy to describe. When we could reach that state, the feeling was of complete peace and harmony."

# ALPHA step A3: Diffusion of meditative practices

## Report 2: Sustainability decision checklists

In order to determine the extent to which ALPHA's business practices and mindsets reflected ethical and sustainable business standards, we asked the company's managers to take a short survey on sustainability mindsets. The results revealed that little attention was paid to these work aspects during the daily grind and associated business pressures. The survey's authors incorporated decision dilemmas, and many ALPHA managers chose options that reflected short-sighted, aggressive business tactics as opposed to more forward-looking and socially responsible ones. As a consequence—and in light of research results indicating that meditation practices increase the development of sustainability mindsets—the meditation program was expanded company-wide.

Additionally, simple sustainability checklists were utilized to evaluate business decisions. The checklist required a quick assessment of the impact on any stakeholder group, the environment, or the ethical dimension, and their mandated use helped shape business decisions towards a CSR-inclined mindset.

Additional steps taken at this stage included:

- The introduction of the ALPHA Wellbeing and Health Department
- A program to strengthen administrative support processes
- Social employee events
- Value chain development meetings with suppliers focusing on environmental considerations
- Social reporting
- Redesign of specific products

## ALPHA step A4: Embedding meditative practices into business processes

### Report 3: New rules for business meetings

Interventions associated with the second and third steps generated positive results in the corporate culture after six months: (i) the number of regular meditators increased steadily which led to noticeable improvements in ALPHA's business; (ii) the number of open conflicts and arguments in meetings decreased; (iii) stress-related tensions were visibly less than before, despite workloads continuing to be high; and (iv) job satisfaction surveys showed score increases for more than a third of ALPHA's workforce. Motivated by these positive developments, the management team decided to take the next step and embed reflective and meditative practices into business processes. The designated unit (for piloting this development) was the marketing department; ultimately, nine out of its 15 members became regular and experienced meditators.

As a first step, the protocols for meetings were modified for a number of pilot organizations. Each meeting now started with a brief meditation session or a reflective exercise (for those who preferred not to meditate) in order to get into a state of balance and "tune in" to the energies of other participants before discussions started. Some feared that this would be a waste of the scarcest resource: time. However, it actually had the opposite effect: the associated meetings (in which these new protocols were exercised for about ten minutes) had a significant decrease in heated debates and greater focus on consensus decisions (which reduced the net duration of the meetings by an average of 15 minutes). Additionally, the level of creativity increased, which led to spontaneously creative solutions that came "out of the blue." After three months, this practice was expanded company-wide.

ALPHA's leadership and employees began to recognize the significance of implementing a mixture of cognitive and targeted change initiatives. Thus, the aforementioned interventions snowballed into an iterative process of evolution based on direct experience and experimentation, which affected ALPHA's corporate culture and ultimately its business decisions. Subtle individual and collective energies improved across the company, which was able to progress from its L-shape to a state of balance. As a W-shaped corporation, all departments now progressed (at different speeds) and attained a state of cooperation and coordination—in an aligned way.

The next and last step was to attempt a transition from a W- to an M-shape (i.e., flourishing) corporation, by integrating the common good of all stakeholders via the use of collective consciousness (which was used by an increasing number of employees on a regular basis).

## ALPHA step B4: Supporting a collective shift towards flourishing

At this stage, ALPHA had already significantly progressed towards attaining flourishing cultural change, with meditative practices now part of its organizational culture. Targeted change interventions addressed critical aspects of the business model; as a consequence, social integration improved dramatically on multiple levels. Business results started to improve steadily and employee satisfaction continued to increase. At this stage, ALPHA began to extend its focus to stakeholders. Communication with customers and suppliers had already improved and now further steps were taken to incorporate them into strategic decisions:

### Report 4: Stakeholder strategy involvement

The central management team decided that it was time to bring the company's stakeholders closer to its core. Since many actions over the past 1½ years supported its internal stakeholders, they decided to follow our suggestion and focus on wholesale customers, suppliers, the city community, and some relevant NGOs in their industry. The first meeting started with a new protocol: meditation. The formal agenda was subsequently addressed—one item after another. This process was guided by intuition that was enabled via the activation of the catalytic energy and the silence and inspiration of thoughtless awareness. The team ultimately decided that questionnaires, open days, and any type of non-committal consultation were insufficient for achieving the sustainability goals it had set for itself. They decided to establish an advisory group, which could potentially turn into a steering committee. This key step would extend the boundaries of the organization and enable the involvement of the company's most relevant stakeholder groups in its strategic decisions.

In preparation for this, a multi-stakeholder event was organized and representatives of the associated stakeholder groups were invited. At the one-day event (with around 70 external participants), ALPHA presented its new business concepts as well as insights into its corporate culture. Stakeholder representatives were invited to engage with the central management team via working groups and focused on specific topics: improving value chains upstream and downstream, community engagement, CSR, and environment-related issues.

This development put ALPHA on a very different page in terms of its evolutionary development. All stakeholder groups unanimously supported the new strategy, which had a positive impact on ALPHA's external relationships. A survey revealed that both suppliers and customers felt they now had a closer relationship with ALPHA than with its competitors, thus accelerating their desire for long-term cooperation despite being in a very fast-moving industry. Common meditation and introspection experiences also enabled exchanges on a non-material basis and broadened the collective consciousness—in ALPHA and even within the stakeholder groups. Thus, ALPHA flourished together with its stakeholders.

## Example 2: WohnStatt (J-shape)

CEL was solicited to help a company in northern Germany; this relationship would ultimately lead its CEO to state: "The wind of change has surely helped to blow away the cobwebs from the organization and has made us the most dynamic public company in our state."

With about 600 employees, WohnStatt's business consisted of restoring and managing urban housing estates. The company was still publicly owned; however, in accordance with a change in the political landscape several months before our involvement, it was envisioned to be run like a private enterprise, removing direct political influences on the operations of the company. An additional factor was that, since the success of the business was an important measure of success for municipal housing management, WohnStatt's activities were carefully monitored by a number of political players.

The structure of the organization had always been hierarchical. The leaders enjoyed their positions as highly respected individuals with great internal power. Positions and ranks within the company were occupied mainly in accordance with formal qualifications. Performance played a minor role in internal promotions. The company's culture had always been strongly affected by the fact that it had once been a direct part of its urban administration. This history was deeply embedded within the genetic code of the organization, where bureaucratic processes had always played a key role. These characteristics hampered the attainment of the new requirements to deliver highest service standards comparable with the private sector.

The CEO thus decided to further centralize the company by moving the previously dispersed offices into one building. (The organization had previously been organized into regional divisions—each with their own group of customers.) Staff members reacted negatively to the centralization. As soon as they had moved into the new building, the organization was further restructured.

A "one-stop shop" service structure was introduced. For example, the service division was supposed to take over the management of all customer-related communications and procedures—including technical information, which was far outside its understanding. Furthermore, there was an extreme lack of trust among the divisions (e.g., the relationship between the technical and service departments was negatively affected by the firm's track record of poor customer service). The firm's management thus asked us to assist when it became obvious that the transfer of knowledge from the prior to the new service personnel had included longstanding frustrations, which negatively impacted the newly hired personnel.

## WohnStatt step A1: Diagnosis

Not surprisingly, we quickly uncovered the strong J-shape nature of the company and excessive focus on administrative processes, passive and bureaucratic attitudes, as well as the frustration present among staff members. Nevertheless, change was considered dangerous and highly unwelcome. To a lesser extent, we also saw this among many contractors with agreements dating back to when the organization was fully integrated within the city administration and employees essentially could not be fired.

The labor union further slowed down change processes; thus, only top managers had a high degree of willingness to introduce productive changes. Therefore, the decision-making process was slow, formalistic, and inefficient. Additionally, decisions were not formalized via proper control processes. Not surprisingly, frustration and dissatisfaction-induced stress prevailed throughout the organization.

## WohnStatt steps A2 and A3: Meditative practices and diffusion

Report 5: Integrating meditative practices into the training program

At the beginning of the intervention, management was looking for standard change initiatives and management training support. However, when the company's leadership was introduced to our approach, they agreed to allow the inclusion of:

- Reflective and meditative practices to be presented in business workshops on leadership for middle management
- Teambuilding—particularly for the newly formed divisions, customer management, and newcomers in the service department
- Individual coaching for senior management

In this case, the second and third steps were delivered in an integrated way; however, meditation was not introduced directly across the entire organization during the initial stage.

Participation in the workshops on reflective processes was initially hesitant; however, after the initial sessions, word got around that the trainings were helpful and fun. Employee participation picked up; soon, the workshops became standard across the organization. Only a few of the long-serving employees remained doubtful (i.e., more or less negatively inclined towards the program). On the other hand, a small group of employees appreciated this form of exercise—to the extent that they started to practice meditation outside their work environments. The first "clusters" of meditators were thus formed.

Approximately one year later, the positive impact on the business had become clear. A new team spirit had arisen in certain departments that had leaders who had participated in the workshops and introduced different approaches in order to actively motivate (vs. simply control) their subordinates. Still, rewards had be introduced in creative, informal ways at the time, since the municipal-oriented payment structure did not allow for performance-oriented pay structures.

Leaders also initiated peer processes to discuss issues and exchange best practices. Additionally, several other initiatives were introduced during the first two years of the intervention, including:

- Workshops for technicians on environmentally friendly and cost-effective ways of renovating their apartments
- Communication coaching—which included remote training
- Reevaluation of forms and administrative processes (with the intention of reducing paperwork)
- The introduction of a young "high-potential employees" support program
- Internal innovation competitions

In a relatively short time, the firm successfully moved away from a myriad of dated business processes. In fact, after two full years of interventions, approximately 300 employees had participated (at least once) in meditation exercises, and WohnStatt had shifted from a J-shape to a moderate L-shape organization. Based on our experience, this is the usual path taken by J-organizations that are beginning to manage previously overwhelming administrative processes. A state of balance can be achieved once passiveness is transcended and productivity levels rise. Thus, moving from a J- to an L-shape is an important first step. Not surprisingly, business results also improved, putting the corporation ahead of any other comparable company in the context of municipal housing.

At the same time, several important questions had yet to be addressed. The most significant at this stage were:

- How to generate balanced perspectives within top managers (to help them understand that keeping up the current pace would eventually burn out the company)
- How to initiate a knowledge transfer system, involving the whole organization, to support change processes that had already been initiated
- How to motivate and get all employees on board, while defusing frustrated veteran opinion leaders
- How to deal with team members who opposed such changes
- How to better align the flow of communication between the technical and service departments and promote a state of motivation and trust
- How to change bureaucratic attitudes that did not support the higher vision of the company and its reinvigorated business processes
- How to remain economically strong—even when coping with apartments that had been left vacant (due to inadequate allocation processes)

## WohnStatt step A4: Embedding meditative practices in core processes

At this stage, top management agreed to try out alternative ways to move forward since they were motivated by the positive results of the interventions, as well as the significant challenges they were still facing

Report 6: Breaking up decision-making processes

The decision-making protocol within WohnStatt was often limiting, time-consuming, and costly; required that large teams undertake extensive analyses, even when the best solutions were sometimes obvious; and was kept alive out of fear of personal accountability by decision-makers—and as a kind of misunderstood professionalism. However, it was no secret that even when all of the due processes and analyses were followed, success was not a guarantee.

The leadership team accepted our suggestion to allow experimentation with intuitive decisions. Not surprisingly, this began with smaller decisions that did not exceed €5,000 in monetary value. We felt that acceptance of balanced intuition—and allowing space for inspiration and serendipity—could reduce the workload of stressed managers and employees. The newly acquired time would then open up opportunities to breathe, reflect creatively, and engage in internal knowledge transfer, which were all too often forsaken during the "normal" flow of business in the past.

While some leaders refused to participate in the experiment, the manager of a service division (and a strong supporter of balancing practices using meditation) motivated his staff to use these techniques to increase their creative and spontaneous potential. The first intuitive decisions were reported after approximately six weeks; the evaluations, after three months, revealed that no mistakes had been made. The quality of the decision-making in this department remained consistent—despite the fact that substantially less time was invested in making decisions.

WohnStatt's management initiated a project to reduce unnecessary formal steps around decision-making processes. Although spontaneous decision-making was never openly endorsed, it was informally encouraged—particularly by employees who participated in the company-wide reflection and meditation sessions voluntarily.

Over time, meditation became a normal part of work life for many at WohnStatt and clearly had significant positive effects on the corporate culture. Many employees now frequently experienced joy at work—and it proved to be infectious to some extent. Interestingly, many recalcitrant veterans were ultimately sidelined as they lost influence in the organization.

With these developments, a lot of pressure was removed and the shift towards integration could be felt throughout the organization.

> **Experiences by meditators**
>
> "I didn't have any expectation about the entire training. I did it out of curiosity and I never expected I would 'walk this way.' It changed me from the beginning; it's still working inside me and I'm sure I will grow up from this in a more concentrated and conscious way."
>
> "My colleagues notice I'm more relaxed, more satisfied and also more spontaneous."
>
> "Compared with a month ago, I feel more balanced, empathetic towards others, I take things more calmly, and [am] less focused on the very short term ([i.e.,] I have a broader and longer-term vision of things). I also believe that the quality of my relationships with others greatly improved."
>
> "I think we should increase the knowledge and practice of meditation at the collective level. Many ignore it completely."
>
> "These sessions have really helped me to understand people around me better and helped me understand the limits of my work/responsibility and not to take over-responsibility, which was earlier ruining my perspective towards things in life and was making me feel unhappy."

The greatest challenge was to make this experience visible outside the organization as well.

## WohnStatt step B4: Involving stakeholders

### Report 7: Customer–supplier link

Over time, it became evident that improvements in technical support for customers were requiring a relatively significant amount of time.

This was partly due to the culture within the technical department and partly due to the relatively poor relationship between the technical and service departments. Interestingly, an employee in the operations department then made the spontaneous decision to send service requests from property managers and customers simultaneously to the technical department and to the most relevant suppliers. As a result, (i) the suppliers could make offers for parts immediately, (ii) the technicians were notified about the availability of necessary parts (before they even had to look for them), and (iii) the waiting time for the customer was reduced substantially.

Once all of the stakeholders involved in this process discovered the benefits of this new process, regular meetings were introduced; they included property managers, customer representatives, technicians, suppliers, and service staff. Before long, the meetings were promoting further innovations within repair cycles, the relationships between the different groups were improving, and stakeholder awareness (including regarding internal innovations) was increasing.

This initiative greatly affected an environmental project initiated by WohnStatt and a wholesaler that involved the systematic replacement of environmentally unfriendly plastic floors by bamboo-based ones. Large orders helped to reduce the cost of the parts and a new installation technique made the exchange less time-consuming, which benefited the environment, stakeholder relationships, and corporate performance at the same time.

Report 8: The union reunion
The company's relationship with the labor union was perceived by WohnStatt's management as highly problematic due to enduring issues of conflict and lack of trust. Tensions increased further with the initiation of the change process; the union tried to protect employee interests, fearing that any change would be detrimental to the employee population. Frustrated veterans within the organization further fueled this negative atmosphere.

A gradual shift in the relationship began to occur via the company's employee training programs. The more WohnStatt invested in measures to support its staff via social activities and stress management programs, the more difficult it became for union hardliners to find flaws with the new initiative. This supportive environment created a shift in the relationships and the union increasingly considered their relationship with the company's management team to be more of a partnership.

At this stage, the atmosphere in the organization—in terms of employer–employee relationships—had changed substantially. This provided a platform for more meaningful interactions and a true partnership. Eventually, the deputy head of the labor union, on a fact-finding mission, joined the meditation sessions and found no reason to oppose their proliferation throughout the company.

Thus, the initially negative feelings between management and the union improved. The union leader was asked about the reasons for this change and stated: "We are on the side of the employees and protect their rights. In the case of WohnStatt that is an increasingly easy job, since the management seems to have read the writing on the wall and is now working along the same lines."

The examples presented in this chapter will, of course, vary from organization to organization; however, they illustrate a number of potential developments along the proposed implementation process. Based on our experience, the main success factors are (i) the readiness of relevant company leaders to enable this type of evolution, (ii) openness for an unbiased evaluation of the results, and (iii) engagement in the relevant training exercises in order to facilitate the unfolding of the evolutionary processes.

There is enormous potential for research and samples to become statistically more significant if such initiatives are conducted on a larger scale; the scaling-up of applied research will largely depend on the interest and action of corporations and institutional partners.

# Conclusions

"It's a funny thing about life; if you refuse to accept anything but the best, you very often get it."

**Somerset Maugham**

In the previous chapters, we constructed a conceptual puzzle with various elements that must be developed in order for a flourishing organization to emerge. In Chapters 4 and 5, we explored the role of introspective and meditative practices as transformational engines in evolutionary processes at the level of the individual. Chapter 6 then took us through a conceptual journey of the evolutionary processes towards the emergent features of flourishing organizations. In Chapter 7, we then discussed how the actual challenge of initiating and diffusing a change process can be approached. Throughout these chapters, we have tried to paint a landscape of how corporations can mutate into agents of positive change in the evolution of business ecosystems.

Equipped with this awareness and the understanding of how this change can take place, let us now return to the systemic context which provides the backdrop to this unfolding drama. This can help put in perspective the reason why we simply have no choice but to activate this potential in an enlightened manner.

In the words of one of the thought leaders of today's management academia:

> To develop transformational capability, we cannot be normal people doing normal things. We must stand outside the norm. To do that we need to go inside ourselves and ask who we are, what we stand for, and what impact we really want to have. Within ourselves we find principle, purpose, and courage. There we find the capacity not only to withstand the pressures of the external system but also actually to transform the external system. We change the world by changing ourselves.[90]

In the modern day, economic actors largely call the shots. In the second half of the 20th century, enterprises have assumed increasingly significant roles and responsibilities in the management of world affairs. Experts, analysts, and the public all claim that improving the corporate world is a *sine qua non* condition for improving the world. On this new playing field, "business as usual" can no longer be the usual way of doing business. While corporate strategies, organizational practices, and business processes come and go, the mindset of decision-makers has by and large remained stable over time. While we acknowledge that this often makes a lot of sense, the current systemic and organizational challenges worldwide necessitate a mindset change.

## Back to the systemic challenge

> "You cannot escape the responsibility of tomorrow by evading it today."
>
> **Abraham Lincoln**

The mechanism of Adam Smith's "invisible hand" rests on the assumption that whatever works for me works for everyone else. This ego-centered consciousness has worked well enough for capitalism, generating wealth and progress at increasing speeds throughout the past two centuries. However, it has also created private entities with powers larger than those of states (and limited accountability, let alone representative legitimacy), powered by the force of greed. This trend has triggered significant inequalities in income distribution and has helped bring the global ecological system to the brink of disaster.

We have been warned that capitalism is the gateway to a doomsday scenario—a core tenet of the Marxist doctrine. However, while the resilience of capitalism seems to have proven its critics wrong thus far, false alarms do not preclude a real one. In fact, it is plain to see that when the public interest is sacrificed, so is the private interest of all. Furthermore, the cost of the old pattern of doing business (and related economic externalities) has proven to be ruinous.

Then it came: the Great Recession. As states bailed out the banks in the 2007–2009 financial meltdown, they did so via the socialization of debt in such an iniquitous manner that the public was left aghast. Confidence in policymakers was by and large shattered. Open democracy activists demanded that mainstream economic models (and the policies constructed upon them) be overhauled and that a reformed financial system, with new rules for governing corporations, be rapidly adopted. However, large-scale protests came and went without visible impact on how we go about doing business.

Today, the public mind appears to still be acutely focused on income inequality and opportunities for improving living standards. The 80 wealthiest people in the world own, at present, the same amount of wealth as the poorest half of the world's population. Interestingly, it has never been the case in the past that individuals could even be wealthier than the state. People are hurt and their anger is further intensified via the social media, instantaneous communication, and information technologies. Those who play are not those who pay—and the mounting indignation deeply affects the political landscapes in industrial countries. In his time, Roosevelt warned us that "poverty anywhere is a threat to prosperity everywhere."

And yet, we have fallen into the spiral of increasing wealth disparity. At the same time, growing anger, political polarization, and religious fundamentalism are destabilizing the geopolitical status quo. In turn, migrations towards "wealthy" states prime the success of populist formations in richer countries. Such trends erect barriers to trade and the freedom of movement. Debt and refugee crises, such as witnessed in the recent Greek tragedy, poignantly remind us of the difficulties we face in addressing such vicious cycles.

In this book, we have explored one possible solution to addressing some aspects of this systemic challenge. We have proposed a way to bring forth profound changes in the social contract that links private enterprises with the local, national, and global communities they serve—via transformations at the individual, organizational, societal, and environmental levels.

## Back to the evolutionary challenge

> "Organizations willing to innovate and to work with government to raise the bar across their industries are essential for reaching tipping points where snowball effects create exponential positive change."[91]
>
> Peter Senge

Today, alert thinkers recognize the intricate correlations between individual and collective transformations. Much of movement—in nature, society, or business—is about evolutionary patterns. As a species, we are propelled forward by the inexorable force of the evolutionary dynamic which has brought us to this stage and is pushing us into the future—seemingly at an exponential pace. This is the same power that is compelling us to evolve our business environment, which is increasingly becoming a single entity spanning the planet. The key question is whether we will find a way to recognize and align ourselves with this evolutionary power—or swim against the current.

We have submitted that personal development must be viewed holistically, as the individual is a complex interweaving of the physical, mental, emotional, and spiritual selves. Underneath these dimensions is an invisible energetic network, which keeps the body healthy, sustains our mental abilities, nourishes our emotions, and helps us to fulfill our purpose and attain our goals. Likewise, an organization's health and functionality rests on a variety of interlocked aspects: administrative, operational, and strategic.

The inner integration of the individual makes possible the outer integration of the corporation. The W-shape generates stability and resilience and overcomes the corresponding inconsistencies and wastes of resources. The adaptive capacity and safe haven of a balanced state reflected by the W-shape also provide a competitive advantage when managing risk.

As a corporation progressively graduates from the W- to the M-shape, the integration of evolved aptitudes transcends the mere thought or organizational constructs that its members can come up with while trying to find a middle-ground solution. The response is wider than just its mental component. It draws its wisdom from a deeper linkage to the collective unconscious with which we become connected when our catalytic energy is awakened and our seventh center becomes activated.

The positive ramifications of such a shift into an expanded consciousness—and the manifestation of a flourishing organization—can be viewed as a compact with the future. Months and years later, its beneficial influence will continue to nourish self-feeding innovative processes for all parties involved. Instead of a transaction with benefits derived from balancing the pros and cons within a "box," a flourishing organization reaches "outside the box" and into the broader field of altruistic action, connectivity, and subsequently serendipity—sowing seeds for great things ahead.

The attainment of sustainability-as-flourishing in individuals and organizations means that the heart opens within the brain of the doer—guiding the best possible course of action for all parties involved. The path towards progress comes to us via our intuition—an inspiration that dawns upon us from the collective unconscious.

In a nutshell, flourishing M-shape corporations can generate a new world with enhanced values because, in the words of Shri Mataji Nirmala Devi, they represent and foster "the flowering of the whole, of which we are a part and parcel." In this expanded range of achievements we can expect to reap beneficial collateral effects that extend well beyond the corporation itself.

The M-shape is the stage where capitalism can truly unleash its enormous potential for global flourishing. We are coming full circle to realize the soundness of the ground premise of capitalism: "what is good for me is good for you." At the same time, in this new logic of integration we also realize the premise of socialism: "what is good for you is good for me." While such considerations sound theoretical, the reality of this transformation can be apprehended only at a direct experimental level. This is because our own reality goes beyond fiction.

In George Lucas's epochal "Star Wars" franchise, Yoda tells Luke Skywalker about the power that pervades everything and flows within all. He tells him: "Use the Force!" But when Luke, after his own unsuccessful attempts, sees Yoda raising his star cruiser immersed in the swamp with the sole power of his mind, he exclaims "I can't believe it!" Yoda aptly notes: "This is why you fail."

The only belief that works is the one borne by experience. On that basis, we submit that we have experienced the power we harness, not by concentrating the mind like Master Yoda but by bringing it into thoughtless awareness. In a way, this is indeed a better way of connecting with "the Force." After all, the universal unconscious keeps sending inspiration to filmmakers, writers, and scientists when they touch the state of collective consciousness. The decoding is up to us.

"Adapt or perish" is the motto that rules the living—from amoebae to human civilizations. Adaptation is about daring to make new choices and experiment. If one assumes that an individual survives because of his or her capacity to evolve, then destruction would naturally result from an incapacity to evolve and change. This may apply to any individual, organization, corporation, or society that loses its connection to the third, central channel.

This is the thought we would like to live you with. Daring to choose the path towards your and your colleagues' evolutionary leap. Experimenting with inner experiences that endow us with capacities and aptitudes we did not even think could exist. Supporting our communities of colleagues and business partners, of friends and family, taking up the challenge of making the world a flourishing garden. And seeing it happen before your eyes, as you stroll from home to work, and back home, every day a little more clearly, vividly, unmistakably.

There is nothing better than your own experience when you perceive these subtle and yet deep, fundamental changes. We wish you, dear reader, to enjoy the leap and flourish well!

# Glossary

**Aptitude center.** One of seven energy centers located along the spine and in the brain, embodying various human aptitudes and corresponding on the physical level to nervous plexuses.

**Catalytic energy.** Located in the sacrum bone normally in a dormant state, it can activate an inner transformation through the parasympathetic nervous system which includes the enabling of collective consciousness in the individual.

**Chakra.** See *Aptitude center*.

**Collective consciousness.** The ability to feel or register others on one's central nervous system.

**Flourishing at individual level.** Development of aptitudes or virtues to the fullest potential, realizing a state of completeness in the way we perceive and connect to ourselves and the rest of the world.

**Flourishing organization.** An organization that has reached a state of collective consciousness in which decisions and actions are geared to nurture and realize the development of the fullest potential for all the actors in the socio-economic and natural system.

**J-shaped corporation.** An organization with a significant preponderance of administrative functions (left SNS) over productive functions.

**L-shaped corporation.** An organization with a significant preponderance of productive functions (right SNS) over administrative functions.

**M-shaped corporation.** See *Flourishing organization*.

**Meditation as a practice.** A method of personal development with many definitions and variations, referred to in this book as a practice based on the awakening of the catalytic energy which subsequently facilitates the state of thoughtless awareness.

**Meditation as a state.** See *Thoughtless awareness*.

**PNS (parasympathetic nervous system).** The part of the involuntary nervous system that serves to slow the heart rate, increase intestinal and glandular activity, and relax the sphincter muscles.

**SNS (sympathetic nervous system).** A part of the nervous system that serves to accelerate the heart rate, constrict blood vessels, and raise blood pressure. It has a left-side (emotions, desires, past) and a right-side (mental and physical activity) component which have complementary qualities and functions.

**Thoughtless awareness.** An elevated state of consciousness achieved through certain methods of meditation, which is characterized by the absence of thoughts coupled with heightened perception.

**W-shaped corporation.** An organization that has achieved a certain degree of balance between productive (right SNS) and administrative functions (left SNS).

# Bibliography

Aftanas, L., Golocheikine, S., "Human anterior and frontal midline theta and lower alpha reflect emotionally positive state and internalized attention: High-resolution EEG investigation of meditation." *Neuroscience Letters* 310(1) (2001): 57-60.

Aftanas, L., Golocheikine, S., "Non-linear dynamic complexity of the human EEG during meditation." *Neuroscience Letters* 330 (2002): 143-146.

Aftanas, L, Golosheikin, S., "Changes in cortical activity in altered states of consciousness: The study of meditation by high-resolution EEG." *Human Physiology* 29(2) (2003): 143-151.

Aftanas, L., Golosheykin, S., "Impact of regular meditation practice on EEG activity at rest and during evoked negative emotions." *International Journal of Neuroscience* 115(6) (2005): 893-909.

Benson, H., Klipper, M.Z., *The Relaxation Response*. New York: HarperCollins, 2000.

Blair, M., Stout, L., "A team production theory of corporate law," *Virginia Law Review* 85(2) (March 1999).

Cavagnaro, E., Curiel G., *The Three Levels of Sustainability*. Sheffield, UK: Greenleaf Publishing, 2012.

Chandler, A., *Strategy and Structure: Chapters in the History of the American Industrial Enterprise*. Frederick, MD: Beard Books, 1962.

Churchland, P.S., *Neurophilosophy. Towards a Unified Science of the Mind/Brain*. Cambridge, MA: MIT Press, 1989: 482.

Collins, J., *Good to Great: Why Some Companies Make the Leap, and Others Don't*. New York: Harper Business, 2001.

De Geus A., *The Living Company*. Boston, MA: Longview Publishing, 2002.

De Kalbermatten, G., *The Third Advent*. New York: Daisy America, 2003.

Dusek, J.A., Out, H.H., Wohlhueter, A.L., Bhasin, M., Zerbini, L.F., Joseph, M.G., et al., "Genomic counter-stress changes induced by the relaxation response." *PLoS ONE* 3(7) (2008): e2576. doi:10.1371/journal.pone.0002576.

Ehrenfeld, J., Hoffman, A., *Flourishing: A Frank Conversation about Sustainability.* Redwood, CA: Stanford University Press, 2013.

Elkington J., *Cannibals with Forks: The Triple Bottom Line of Twenty-First Century Business.* Oxford, UK: Capstone, 1997.

Ferri, I., *Meditazione, Yoga e Scienza Medica.* Italy: Cultura Della Madre, 2012.

Freeman, E., Wicks, A.C., Parmar, B., "Stakeholder Theory and 'The Corporate Objective Revisited'", *Organization Science* 15(3) (2004): 3 64-369.

Freeman, E. et al., *Stakeholder Theory: The State of the Art.* New York: Cambridge University Press, 2010.

Giddens, A., *Central Problems in Social Theory: Action, Structure, and Contradiction in Social Analysis.* Oakland, CA: University of California Press, 1979.

Gladwell, M., *Blink: The Power of Thinking without Thinking.* Back Bay Books, 2007.

Goleman, D., *Emotional Intelligence: Why It Can Matter More Than IQ.* Munich: Carl Hanser Verlag, 1996.

Gore, A., *An Inconvenient Truth.* New York: Rodale, 2006.

Hackl, W., "Effects of Sahaja Yoga on selected psychological factors. An empiric research with emphasis on personality structure, reduction of anxiety, drug abuse and cognitive ability." University of Vienna, 1996.

Harrison, L., Rubia, K., Manocha, R., "Sahaja Yoga meditation as a family treatment program for attention deficit hyperactivity disorder children." *Clinical Child Psychology and Psychiatry* 9(4) (2003): 479-497.

Hernández, S.E., Suero, J., Rubia, K., González-Mora, J.L., "Monitoring the neural activity of the state of mental silence while practicing Sahaja yoga meditation." *Journal of Alternative and Complementary Medicine* 21(3) (March 2015): 175-179.

Hernández, S.E., Suero, J., Barros, A., González-Mora, J.L., Rubia, K., "Increased grey matter associated with long-term Sahaja Yoga Meditation: A Voxel-Based Morphometry study." *PLoS ONE* 11(3) (2016): e0150757. doi:10.1371/journal.pone.0150757.

Hofstede, G., *Culture's Consequences.* Sage Publishing, 1984

Jung, C.G., *The Archetypes and the Collective Unconscious.* Princeton, NJ: Princeton University Press, 1981.

Jung, C.G., *Die Beziehungen zwischen dem Ich und dem Unbewußten.* Munich: DTV, 2001.

Koltko-Rivera, M.E., "Rediscovering the later version of Maslow's hierarchy of needs: Self-transcendence and opportunities for theory, research, and unification." *Review of General Psychology* 10(4) (December 2006): 302-317.

*Kuang Tzu.* Trans. James Legge and arranged by Clare Waltham; New York: ACE Books, 1971.

Lacy, P., Rutqvist J., *Waste to Wealth.* New York: Palgrave Macmillan, 2015.

Laloux, F., *Reinventing Organizations.* Nelson Parker, 2014.

Lao Tzu, *Tao Te Ching.* CreateSpace Independent Publishing Platform, 2013.

Laszlo, C., Brown, J., *The Flourishing Enterprise: The New Spirit of Business.* Stanford University Press, 2014.

Mackey, J., Sisodia R., *Conscious Capitalism*. Boston, MA: Harvard Business School Publishing, 2013.

Manocha, R., Gordon, A., Black, D., Malhi, G., "Using meditation for less stress and better wellbeing: A seminar for GPs." *Australian Family Physician* 38(6) (June 2009).

Manocha, R., *Silence Your Mind*. Australia: Hachette Publishing, 2013.

Mao Tse Tung, *On Contradiction*, August 1937.

Marino, Eduardo, *Science: A Way to Spirituality*. Italy: Cultura della Madre, 2015.

Maslow, A., *Towards a Psychology of Being*. New York: John Wiley, 1968.

Meadows D., *Thinking in Systems: A Primer*. White River Junction, VT: Chelsea Green Publishing, 2008.

Mishra. R., Barlas, C., Barone, D., "Plasma beta endorphin levels in humans: Effect of Sahaja Yoga." Paper presented at the "Medical Aspects of Sahaja Yoga" medical conference, New Delhi, India, 1993

OECD, *In It Together: Why Less Inequality Benefits Growth*. Report, May 2015.

Pink, D., *A Whole New Mind: Why Right-Brainers Will Rule the Future*. Riverhead Books, 2006.

Quinn R., *Change the World: How Ordinary People Can Accomplish Extraordinary Results*. San Francisco: Jossey-Bass, 2000.

Rajan, R.G., Zingales, L., *Saving Capitalism from the Capitalists*. Princeton, NJ: Princeton University Press, 2004.

Rifkin, J., *The Empathic Civilization: The Race to Global Consciousness in a World in Crisis*. TarcherPerigee, 2009.

Rifkin, J., *The Zero Marginal Cost Society: The Internet of Things, the Collaborative Commons, and the Eclipse of Capitalism*. St. Martin's Griffin, 2015.

Rubia, K., "The neurobiology of meditation and its clinical effectiveness in psychiatric disorders." *Biological Psychology* 82 (2009): 1–11.

Scharmer, O., Kaufer, K., *Leading from the Emerging Future: From Ego-System to Eco-System Economies*. San Francisco: Berrett-Koehler Publishers, 2013.

Senge P., *The Necessary Revolution*. Broadway Books, 2008.

Senge, P., Scharmer, O., Jaworsky, J., Flowers, B.S., *Presence*. New York: Random House, 2005.

Sisodia, R., Sheth, J., Wolfe, D., *Firms of Endearment*. Philadelphia: Wharton School Publishing, 2007.

Stiglitz, J., Greenwald, B., *Creating a Learning Society*. New York: Columbia University Press, 2014.

Stout, L., *The Shareholder Value Myth: How Putting Shareholders First Harms Investors, Corporations, and the Public*. San Francisco: Berrett-Koehler Publishers, 2012.

Williamson, O.E., *Corporate Control and Business Behavior: An Inquiry into the Effects of Organization Form on Enterprise Behavior*. Englewood Cliffs, NJ: Prentice-Hall, 1970.

Zohar, D., Marshall, I., *Spiritual Capital: Wealth That We Can Live By*. San Francisco: Berrett-Koehler Publishers, 2004.

Zollo, M., Winter, S., "Deliberate learning and the evolution of dynamic capabilities." *Organization Science* 13(3) (2002): 339-351.

# Endnotes

## Introduction
1. Laszlo, C., Brown, J., *The Flourishing Enterprise: The New Spirit of Business*. Stanford University Press, 2014.
2. Ehrenfeld, J., Hoffman, A., *Flourishing: A Frank Conversation about Sustainability*. Redwood, CA: Stanford University Press, 2013.

## Chapter 1: The challenge
3. A "wicked" problem is a problem that is difficult or impossible to solve because of incomplete, contradictory, and changing requirements that are difficult to recognize. "Wicked" is meant in the sense of *resistant to resolution* (vs. "evil"). Moreover, because of complex interdependencies, the effort to solve one aspect of a wicked problem may reveal or create other problems.
4. OECD, *In It Together: Why Less Inequality Benefits Growth*. Report, May 2015.
5. See Waddell, S., Waddock, S., Cornell, S., Dentoni, D., McLachlan, M., Meszoely, G., "Large systems change: An emerging field of transformation and transitions." *Journal of Corporate Citizenship* 58 (2015): 5-30.
6. Meadows D., *Thinking in Systems: A Primer*. White River Junction, VT: Chelsea Green Publishing, 2008.
7. "Flourishing means not only to grow, but to grow well, to prosper, to thrive, to live to the fullest [. . .] we strive for a context in which all life can flourish. [. . .] Flourishing is the realization of a state of completeness [. . .] Flourishing is the result of acting out of caring for oneself, other human beings, the rest of the [. . .] world. [. . .] Sustainability-as-flourishing refers to a state of *Being* in which the individual realizes a sense of wholeness, completion, or perfection," Ehrenfeld and Hoffman, *op. cit.*: 6, 17-18.

8. "Sustainability-as-flourishing challenges us to shift from defining ourselves by the materials we possess—Having—to defining ourselves by the extent to which we act authentically—Being," Ehrenfeld and Hoffman, *op. cit.*: 7.
9. Blair, M., Stout, L., "A team production theory of corporate law," *Virginia Law Review* 85(2) (March 1999). Stout, L., *The Shareholder Value Myth: How Putting Shareholders First Harms Investors, Corporations, and the Public*. San Francisco: Berrett-Koehler Publishers, 2012.
10. For a current overview of the stakeholder theory of the firm, see Freeman, E. et al., *Stakeholder Theory: The State of the Art*. New York: Cambridge University Press, 2010; or a more managerially oriented version in Freeman, E., Wicks, A.C., Parmar, B., "Stakeholder Theory and 'The Corporate Objective Revisited'", *Organization Science* 15(3) (2004): 3 64-369.
11. A flourishing organization is capable of creating value for its stakeholders by enabling the realization of its highest potential through the development of joint purpose, sustainable behaviors, and common value. In short, it is an organization that sustains its own sustainability.
12. Such top-down change initiatives would be typically carried out through controlled experimentation in pilot projects, evidence-based selection of successful experiments, and scaling-up processes throughout the organization and across its stakeholders.
13. The stimulation will most likely take the form of a combination of regulatory and soft-type policy interventions. The appropriate mix of these components will also be determined through controlled experimentation in pilot projects, evidence-based selection, and scaling-up initiatives.

## Chapter 2: The leap in the field

14. Jung, C.G., *Die Beziehungen zwischen dem Ich und dem Unbewußten*. Munich: DTV, 2001.
15. Koltko-Rivera, M.E., "Rediscovering the later version of Maslow's hierarchy of needs: Self-transcendence and opportunities for theory, research, and unification." *Review of General Psychology* 10(4) (December 2006): 302-317.
16. "Corporate mobbing" is a term used to describe a variety of behaviors in the workplace that amount to emotional abuse by workers of a fellow employee or employees.
17. The skin conductance response, also known as the electrodermal response (and in older terminology as "galvanic skin response"), is the phenomenon whereby the skin momentarily becomes a better conductor of electricity when either external or internal stimuli occur that are physiologically arousing.
18. Goleman, D., *Emotional Intelligence: Why It Can Matter More Than IQ*. Munich: Carl Hanser Verlag, 1996: 65, 132.
19. The D2 of Brickenkamp and Zillmer allows for a raw score to range from 0 to 653. It measures at the same time Speed, Errors, Accuracy, Concentration, and Fluctuation.

20. Personal values were assessed through the individual version of the Global Value Survey developed by Shalom Schwartz, and the emotional traits through the PANAS scale.
21. The PANAS/STAI score showed strongest shifts for the post-measurement in being more confident, less upset, less afraid, and less angry. The Guiding Principles of Life test, developed by Shalom Schwartz, showed its highest increase (mean value) on the scale from 1–7 in:
    - Being successful (+1.3)
    - Inner harmony (+1.2)
    - Importance of intelligence (-1.0)
    - Mature love (+0.9)
    - Indulgence (-0.8)
22. Zollo, M., Minoja, M., Casanova, L., Hockerts, K., Neergaard, P., Schneider, S., Tencati, A., "Towards an internal change management perspective of CSR: Evidence from project RESPONSE on the sources of cognitive alignment between managers and their stakeholders, and their implications for social performance." *Corporate Governance*, September 2009.
23. Schneider, S., Zollo, M., Manocha, R., "Developing socially responsible behavior in managers: Experimental evidence on the effectiveness of different approaches to management education." *Journal of Corporate Citizenship* 39 (September 2010).
24. Schneider, Zollo, Manocha, *op. cit.*
25. "Statistical significance" means that a given effect (in this case, the change in the responses to the same questions after the completion of a training intervention) is *not* due to chance, with a probability larger than 95%. Some of the results reported reach significance levels of 99% or better. A "weaker" significance level is considered to be between 90% and 95%.
26. Crilly, D., Schneider, S., Zollo, M., "The psychological antecedents to socially responsible behavior." *European Management Review* 5(3) (August 2008).

## Chapter 3: The neuroscientific evidence

27. Churchland, P.S., *Neurophilosophy. Towards a Unified Science of the Mind/Brain*. Cambridge, MA: MIT Press, 1989: 482.
28. Maslow A., *Towards a Psychology of Being*. New York: John Wiley, 1968. Copyright © 1968, 1999 John Wiley & Sons. All rights reserved.
29. "We are obliged to assume the existence of a collective psychic substratum. I have called this the *collective unconscious*." Jung, C.G., Kerényi, K., *Essays on a Science of Mythology*. Bollingen Series XXII; Princeton, NJ: Princeton University Press, 3rd printing, 1973: 74.
30. Jung, C.G., *Yoga and the West*. In *The Collected Works. Vol. 11: Psychology and Religion—West and East*. Princeton, NJ: Princeton University Press, 2nd edition, 1975: §875, p. 537.
31. This, incidentally, has been popularly received in the West through the imported Sanskrit notion of *nirvana*.

32. Just to give an idea about the importance of dopamine, consider that the main factor causing Parkinson's disease is the lack of sufficient dopamine production and release in specific brain areas.
33. Aftanas, L., Golocheikine, S., "Non-linear dynamic complexity of the human EEG, during meditation." *Neuroscience Letters* 330 (2002): 143-146.
34. Dusek, J.A., Out, H.H., Wohlhueter, A.L., Bhasin, M., Zerbini, L.F., Joseph, M.G., et al., "Genomic counter-stress changes induced by the relaxation response." *PLoS ONE* 3(7) (2008): e2576. doi:10.1371/journal.pone.0002576.
35. Mishra. R., Barlas, C., Barone, D., "Plasma beta endorphin levels in humans: Effect of Sahaja Yoga." Paper presented at the "Medical Aspects of Sahaja Yoga" medical conference, New Delhi, India, 1993.
36. Harrison, L., Rubia, K., Manocha, R., "Sahaja Yoga meditation as a family treatment program for attention deficit hyperactivity disorder children." *Clinical Child Psychology and Psychiatry* 9(4) (2003): 479-497.
37. Manocha, R., Gordon, A., Black, D., Malhi, G., "Using meditation for less stress and better wellbeing: A seminar for GPs." *Australian Family Physician* 38(6) (June 2009).
38. Aftanas, L., Golosheykin, S., "Impact of regular meditation practice on EEG activity at rest and during evoked negative emotions." *International Journal of Neuroscience* 115(6) (2005): 893-909.
39. Aftanas, L., Golocheikine, S., "Human anterior and frontal midline theta and lower alpha reflect emotionally positive state and internalized attention: High-resolution EEG investigation of meditation." *Neuroscience Letters* 310(1) (2001): 57-60. Aftanas and Golocheikine, *op. cit.* (2002). Aftanas, L, Golosheikin, S., "Changes in cortical activity in altered states of consciousness: The study of meditation by high-resolution EEG." *Human Physiology* 29(2) (2003): 143-151.
40. Aftanas and Golosheykin, *op. cit.* (2005).
41. Functional Magnetic Resonance Imaging: a functional neuroimaging procedure using MRI technology which measures brain activity by detecting changes associated with blood flow.
42. Rubia, K., "The neurobiology of meditation and its clinical effectiveness in psychiatric disorders." *Biological Psychology* 82 (2009): 1–11. Hernández, S.E., Suero, J., Rubia, K., González-Mora, J.L., "Monitoring the neural activity of the state of mental silence while practicing Sahaja yoga meditation." *Journal of Alternative and Complementary Medicine* 21(3) (March 2015): 175-179.
43. The yoga/meditation experience was significantly predictive of gray matter volume in many of these same neuroanatomical regions. Study findings suggest that the practice of yoga is associated with enhanced cognitive function coupled with enlargement of brain structures related to higher-order (executive) control capacities. Voxel-Based Morphometry analysis (neuroimaging analysis technique that allows investigation of focal differences in brain anatomy using statistical parametric mapping) indicated that, on the whole, meditators exhibited significantly larger prefrontal cortical regions (e.g., the middle and orbital frontal gyri) than the control group. Experimental studies indicate these

brain structures are mobilized during tasks that involve (i) cognitive control, (ii) inhibition of automated or prepotent responses, (iii) contextually appropriate selection and coordination of actions, and (iv) reward evaluation and decision-making.

44. Self-reported data from the Cognitive Failures Questionnaire (a self-report measure designed to assess mental lapses; Broadbent, D.E., Cooper, P.F., FitzGerald, P., Parkes K.R., "The Cognitive Failures Questionnaire (CFQ) and its correlates." *Journal of Clinical Psychology* 21(1) (February 1982): 1-16) indicate that greater gray matter volume in these regions was associated with making fewer errors in attention, memory, and motor function in everyday tasks. Relative to the control group, long-term meditators also exhibited significantly greater gray matter volume in the cerebellum—a brain structure known, for decades, as essential for the precise coordination and timing of body movements and, more recently, associated with executive functions. Common to both of these domains, the cerebellum may predict the consequences of planned actions (i.e., motor behaviors or mental operations) and use these predictions to update action plans. Putatively, the integration of cognitive and motor control is mediated by anatomical connections between units in the cerebellum and regions of the prefrontal cortex. The fact that the number of years (associated with meditation and yoga experience) was significantly associated with gray matter volume suggests that the duration of yoga practice may contribute, in part, to the observed volumetric differences in brain structure—possibly by stimulating neuroplasticity.

45. Hernández, S.E., Suero, J., Barros, A., González-Mora, J.L., Rubia, K., "Increased grey matter associated with long-term Sahaja Yoga Meditation: A Voxel-Based Morphometry study." *PLoS ONE* 11(3) (2016): e0150757. doi:10.1371/journal.pone.0150757.

46. The sample was composed of a group of 42 graduate business students, of which 12 were randomly allocated to a 16-hour meditation course (four sessions of one hour each for four weeks). Each session included 10–15 minutes of explanation of the new technique and 45–50-minute meditation practices. In addition to the pre–post brain imaging assessments of both activation and structural properties (e.g., gray matter density), the protocol included a battery of psychometric tests related to personality, emotions, and stress/anxiety as well as a weekly self-assessment of extra-sensorial perceptions and wellbeing (see Chapters 4 and 5). The program was financially supported by CARIPLO Foundation. Results were presented at the final symposium held in June 2014. Part of them are in "Short-term Sahaja yoga meditation training modulates brain structure and spontaneous activity in the executive control network" by Alessandra Dodich, Maurizio Zollo, Chiara Crespi, Stefano Cappa, Daniella Laureiro Martinez, Andrea Falini, and Nicola Canessa.

47. The "tragedy of the commons" is an economic theory of a situation within a shared-resource system where individual users acting independently according to their own self-interest behave contrary to the common good of all users

by depleting that resource through the cumulative effect of their individual actions.

## Chapter 4: The inner transformation engine

48. Refer, for instance, to the essay of Brazilian quantum physicist Eduardo Marino, *Science: A Way to Spirituality*. Italy: Cultura della Madre, 2015.
49. Patanjali, *Yoga Sutra* I.2.
50. Swami Svatmarana, *Hatha Yoga Pradipika* III.7(2). Trans. Elsy Becherer; London: Aquarian/Thorsons, 1992.
51. "Just as in the firmament, which covers the whole universe, we behold different shapes formed by the conjunction of stars and planets to make us aware of hidden things and deep mysteries; so upon the skin which covers our body and which is, as it were, the body's firmament, covering all, there are shapes and designs—the stars and planets of the body's firmament, the skin through which the wise of heart may behold the hidden things and the deep mysteries indicated by these shapes and expressed in the human form." *The Zohar*. Translated by Harry Sperling and Maurice Simon; London/New York: The Soncino Press, 1984: II, 76a, Vol. III, p. 231.
52. "Said Rabbi Judah, 'It is not a dictum of the Rabbis that the world rests on seven supports, as it is written, *Wisdom hath hewn out her seven pillars*'? Rabbi Jose replied: 'That is so . . .'," *The Zohar*: I, 82a, Vol. I, p. 274.
53. "It is from this palace that the Pillar in the middle makes all the spirits ascend to the seventh palace, which is the Mystery of mysteries and where all the ladders arrive, since they are united there to form only one." *The Zohar*: I, 45a, in *Sepher Ha-Zohar (Le Livre de la Splendeur)*. Trans. Jean de Pauly; Paris: Éd. G.-P. Maisonneuve et Larose, 1970,: Vol. I, p. 263.
54. "Now after the superior powers had created all these natures . . . they cut various channels through the body as through a garden, that it might be watered as from a running stream. In the first place, they cut two hidden channels or veins down to the back where the skin and the flesh join, which answered severally to the right and left side of the body. These they let down along the backbone, so as to have the marrow of generation between them, where it was most likely to flourish, and in order that the stream coming down from above might flow freely to the other parts, and equalize the irrigation. In the next place, they divided the veins about the head, and interlacing them, they sent them in opposite directions; those coming from the right side they sent to the left of the body, and those from the left they diverted towards the right." Plato, *Timaeus* 77 c–e. In *The Collected Dialogues of Plato*. Bollingen Series LXXI; Princeton, NJ: Princeton University Press, 1961: 1,199.
55. Mair, V.H., *Tao Te Ching*. New York: Bantam Books, 1990: 146-147.
56. Harvalik, Z.V., "Biophysical Magnetometer-Gradiometer." *Virginia Journal of Science* 21(2) (1970): 59-60; cited in Tompkins, P., Bird, C., *The Secret Life of Plants*. New York: Harper & Row, 1973: 302.

57. Tiller, W.A., "Radionics, radiesthesia and physics." In *Proceedings of the Academy of Parapsychology and Medicine, Symposium on the Varieties of Healing Experience*, 1971; cited in Tompkins and Bird, *op. cit.*: 357-358.
58. Mao Tse Tung, *On Contradiction*, August 1937.
59. Benson, H., Klipper, M.Z., *The Relaxation Response*. New York: HarperCollins, 2000.
60. Gravity, generosity of spirit, sincerity, earnestness, and kindness.
61. Manocha, R., *Silence Your Mind*. Australia: Hachette Publishing, 2013.
62. Jung, C.G., *The Psychology of Kundalini Yoga*. Notes of the Seminar Given in 1932 by C.G. Jung; ed. Sonu Shamdasani; Bollingen Series XCIX; Princeton, NJ: Princeton University Press, 1996: Lecture 1, October 12, 1932: 21.
63. Ibid., Lecture 4, November 2, 1932: 68-69.
64. Ehrenfeld and Hoffman, *op. cit.*: 93.
65. Collins, J., *Good to Great: Why Some Companies Make the Leap, and Others Don't*. New York: Harper Business, 2001.
66. Mackey, J., Sisodia R., *Conscious Capitalism*. Boston, MA: Harvard Business School Publishing, 2013: 7.
67. Scharmer, O., Kaufer, K., *Leading from the Emerging Future: From Ego-System to Eco-System Economies*. San Francisco: Berrett-Koehler Publishers, 2013.
68. Sisodia, R., Sheth, J., Wolfe, D., *Firms of Endearment*. Philadelphia: Wharton School Publishing, 2007: 112.
69. Sisodia et al., *op. cit.*: 74.
70. Henry, J., *Creative Management and Development*. London: Sage Publications, 3rd edn, 2006: 17.
71. "Seeing freshly starts with stopping our habitual ways of thinking and perceiving. According to cognitive scientist Francisco Varela, developing the capacity for this sort of stopping involves 'suspension, removing ourselves from the habitual stream of thought'. Varela calls suspension the first basic 'gesture' in in enhancing awareness. [...] By doing so we begin to notice our thoughts and mental models as the working of our own mind. And as we become aware of our thoughts and mental models as the working of our own mind, they begin to have less influence on what we see, Suspension allow us to see our seeing." Senge, P., Scharmer, O., Jaworsky, J., Flowers, B.S., *Presence*. New York: Random House, 2005: 29.
72. Gladwell, M., *Blink: The Power of Thinking without Thinking*. Back Bay Books, 2007.

## Chapter 5: The field of collective consciousness
73. Zaidel, D.W., *Frontiers in Human Neuroscience*, February 2015.
74. Jung and Kerényi, *op. cit.*: 92.
75. Jung, C.G., *The Archetypes and the Collective Unconscious*. Princeton, NJ: Princeton University Press, 1981.
76. Maslow, A., *Towards a Psychology of Being*. New York: John Wiley, 1968: 71.
77. For instance, the claustra below the cerebral cortex or the temporoparietal junction.

78. Beyond sleeping, dreaming, and "awake thinking" consciousness, as mentioned in Chapter 3.
79. *Kuang Tzu*. Trans. James Legge and arranged by Clare Waltham; New York: ACE Books, 1971.
80. See the work of Jeremy Rifkin in *The Empathic Civilization: The Race to Global Consciousness in a World in Crisis*. TarcherPerigee, 2009, and *The Zero Marginal Cost Society: The Internet of Things, the Collaborative Commons, and the Eclipse of Capitalism*. St. Martin's Griffin, 2015.
81. Pink, D., *A Whole New Mind: Why Right-Brainers Will Rule the Future*. Riverhead Books, 2006.

## Chapter 6: The transition models of organizations

82. Such top-down change initiatives would be typically carried out via controlled experimentation in pilot projects, evidence-based selection of successful experiments, and scaling-up processes throughout organizations—and across stakeholders.
83. De Geus A., *The Living Company*. Boston, MA: Longview Publishing, 2002: 201.
84. "Markets need political support, yet their very functioning undermines the support. As a result, the market is a fragile institution, charting a narrow path between the Scylla of overweening government interference and the Charybdis of too little government support." Rajan, R.G., Zingales, L., *Saving Capitalism from the Capitalists*. Princeton, NJ: Princeton University Press, 2004: 313.
85. Williamson refers to this type of organization as a Unitary form, or U-form, corporation. The U-form became dominant at the end of the 19th century and remained dominant through the 1920s. Williamson, O.E., *Corporate Control and Business Behavior: An Inquiry into the Effects of Organization Form on Enterprise Behavior*. Englewood Cliffs, NJ: Prentice-Hall, 1970.
86. Hofstede, G., *Culture's Consequences*. Sage Publishing, 1984.
87. Senge et al., *op. cit.*: 219.
88. Not to be confused with Alfred Chandler's M-form or multi-divisional form (MDF) corporation. Chandler, A., *Strategy and Structure: Chapters in the History of the American Industrial Enterprise*. Frederick, MD: Beard Books, 1962.

## Chapter 7: Practical steps for the transition

89. A triple bottom line measures a company's degree of social responsibility, its economic value and its environmental impact. See Elkington J., *Cannibals with Forks: The Triple Bottom Line of Twenty-First Century Business*. Oxford, UK: Capstone, 1997.

## Conclusions

90. Quinn R., *Change the World: How Ordinary People Can Accomplish Extraordinary Results*. San Francisco: Jossey-Bass, 2000: 19.
91. Senge P., *The Necessary Revolution*. Broadway Books, 2008: 210.